BLACK ANGELS AMONG US

A Quick Start Guide to Angel Investing

Dr. Shante Williams

D1445656

This book is dedicated to all the Angels who have invested in and poured into my life.

To my parents, Kenneth Williams and Pastor Vanessa Whitley, thank you for laying the foundation and encouraging me to keep climbing. To my sisters Tamara Williams and Sade Williams thank you for cheering me on, Team Williams all day. To my nephewson, Kyrie Williams, you are the future and I cannot wait to invest in whatever dreams you have. I love you all!

Be not forgetful to entertain strangers: for thereby some have entertained angels unawares.

HEBREWS 13:2 (KJV)

CONTENTS

INTRODUCTION

B uilding generational wealth is a topic that makes an appearance with growing regularity.

Generational wealth also referred to as "old money," means that the assets built in your lifetime are passed down to your children, grandchildren, and children after them.

The passage of wealth from one generation to another has been discussed from every angle.

Education and entrepreneurship have become the perennial favorites proposed to help the community achieve economic success. However, while education and entrepreneurship are essential components of building wealth, they will not solely aid in building generational wealth.

Education has led to an increase in the professional class within the African American Community. According to the United States Census, since 1940, the percentage of Black Americans over the age of 25 who have attained a high school diploma has steadily increased from 7.7% in 1940 to 87.9% in 2018 (Bureau, 2019).

The number of Black Americans over the age of 25 who have attained a bachelor's degree has also continued to rise from 1.3% in 1940 to 25.2% by 2018 (Bureau, 2019).

However, these educational gains have barely made a dent in closing the wealth gap experienced in this country.

For Black Americans, entrepreneurship has long been a vehicle to gain a sense of independence and freedom by building their own enterprises. These businesses were at one time born out of necessity as there were few businesses that Blacks could patronize and be serviced appropriately. In fact, 1900-1930 is often referred to as the golden age of black entrepreneurship (Walker, 2009).

By 2015, 2.6 million small businesses were owned by Blacks. However, only 4% of these businesses have paid employees, and access to capital is a significant impediment to high growth for many Black-owned small businesses irrespective of the industry.

This speaks to the need for African Americans to not only start businesses, but to also invest in them in order to help achieve new levels of success in the African American business community.

A business that has the ability to grow and scale not only creates jobs, but can create an asset that can last for generations.

Despite the glamorization of entrepreneurship, many have no desire or talent to build a company. But even though we may not all be able to be founders, we can all be OWNERS.

Ownership is key. Ownership, whether it be real estate, or interest in stocks or companies, has helped create wealth that has been passed from one generation to another.

Creating wealth is not merely the act of having an inheritance to give to your children- assets that continue to grow are critical. Once we become fully financially invested in industry and in our communities, then and only then can we say that we are fully invested in the future.

Investors provide capital to businesses. For many of them, that capital is the difference between success and failure. As a result, investors chose winners and, by default, losers.

Those that receive investments are more likely to thrive, and those that do not are more likely to operate in a survival mode that prevents real growth.

According to the Angel Capital Association, only 1.3% of investors are Black. This lack of participation means that many people of color have never even met an active investor and do not know where to start.

Much has been touted about the need to create long-lasting wealth; however, very few guides have shown people of color how to participate in the economy fully.

This guide is intended to give you the information you need to become one of the few black angels that exist in the United States.

In this book, we will discuss how to prepare your finances and lifestyle to become an investor, decide what to invest in, and how to earn investment income.

As a Venture Capitalist and Angel Investor myself, I have deployed capital into many businesses.

My first investment was $1,000 into hair salon products. That investment was small in terms of dollars but outsized in terms of impact. That salon owner was able to put products on her shelves that helped to build a new stream of revenue. She was also able to reinvest the earnings, and use it to drive further growth of her business.

That business now has locations in 2 states, and continues to support a single mother, especially in helping her to pay for her child's college education.

As a Black Angel, I was able to help provide an opportunity for an entrepreneur who had been overlooked by other funders, and certainly not on the radar of traditional Angel Investors.

I genuinely believe that everyone is capable of becoming an investor regardless of your income. The earliest investors in many start-ups and businesses are what I call the 3 F's: Friends, Family, and Fools.

We all are friends and family to someone and this guide will prevent you from being a fool.

I seek to equip a new Army of Black Angels that can move the needle for the Black Community, and create lasting wealth that will mean real freedom for the next generation.

Let's invest together!

PART I: STARTING SOMEWHERE

"Wise spending is part of wise investing. And it's never too late to start."

- Rhonda Katz

Every investor started somewhere. To become an investor, you have to make your first investment but before you can begin the journey, you have to first know where you are.

In this first part, we will discuss:

- Basic terminology
- How to assess where you are
- Preparing your finances for investing
- How to identify what to invest in
- How to seek out the right investments

CHAPTER ONE:
THE BASICS

C apital is the lifeblood of a business. Even the most prosperous businesses need capital injections every now and then to drive growth.

One of the easiest ways for businesses, especially startups, to raise capital is to turn to venture capital firms or Angel investors. But for Black entrepreneurs, raising capital via these sources is almost impossible.

Statistically speaking, the odds are stacked against African-American entrepreneurs.

For instance, reports by CB Insights revealed that only about 1% of Black founders of tech companies receive venture capital funding.

African-American business owners also have a harder time securing loans from banks and traditional financial institutions because many of them are not keen on lending money to minorities.

As a result, African Americans lose out on opportunities to thrive economically, create more employment opportunities for the Black community, and bridge the wealth gap for people of color.

A report released by The Center for Global Policy Solutions revealed that *"there are over 1 million businesses that could be produced by people of color, but are stunted due to socially discriminating financing practices, and a bias towards companies run largely by White men."*

Jessica Norwood, the Founder of The Runway Project Initiative, an organization working to create solutions for addressing the wealth gap impeding minority business growth revealed that *"Many Black entrepreneurs turn to credit cards or moonlighting under part-time or full-time jobs to pad the growth of their business. This bootstrapping method offers drips of money, but makes it much more difficult and time-consuming to access much larger capital"*

A lot of Black business owners, because they cannot access traditional funding like their White counterparts, are left with no choice but to turn to accessible funding like credit cards, which often comes with exorbitant interest rates that they sometimes find very difficult to cope with.

They often end up with huge debt burden, and get pushed further down the rabbit hole of poor credit scores, business collapse, liquidation, and generational poverty.

Some potential founders, not willing to take the risk, simply dump their business ideas and take up paid employment instead.

We owe it to our communities and the future generations to put an end to these socially discriminating financing practices that is making it difficult for the African American business community to grow, thrive, and create any sustainable generational wealth.

We have to step in to save our African American business community, and give Black founders and business owners the opportunity that they are consistently being denied.

The only way we can do this is by becoming investors ourselves.

Only about 1.3% of Angel investors in the United States are African Americans, and this might explain why many Black business owners and founders continue to be marginalized and discriminated against.

If we as African Americans participate more in investing- become Angel Investors ourselves, then we will be able to give more African-Americans the platform to raise capital for their businesses, generate wealth, and create sustainable wealth for the future generations.

One reason why there are so few Black Angel investors is because of the common misconception that you have to be a millionaire, or be very wealthy to become an investor- No, you don't have to.

In fact, with as little as $2,000, you can get started as an individual Angel investor, and with as little as $500, you can join an angel investment group, and invest collectively with other Black Angels.

Imagine thousands of African-Americans coming together, and pulling small amounts of money together for investments- it quickly adds up and can make a significant difference in our community.

For most beginner investors, the terms and terminology can be daunting. Every investment category has its lingo, but there are some underlying basics that you should know.

Who Is An Angel Investor?

An Angel investor, also known as a private investor, seed investor, or angel funder, is generally a high net worth individual who provides financial backing for small startups or entrepreneurs.

This type of Investor is looking for ownership in the startup in exchange for the cash.

The symbolism of an angel is very appropriate. Usually, an angel is investing money when the company is not generating revenue, and needs a miracle because they are in a slow or difficult phase in the company's life.

Angel investors are typically not looking to be involved in the day to day operations of the company, and an angel investor does not have to be an accredited investor; however, many are.

This is where the opportunity for everyone to participate in investing lies as there is no minimum investment for an angel investor.

Even though the average investment for an angel investment is approximately $75,000, DO NOT let this discourage you as this number varies widely depending on what region of the country you occupy.

Types Of Angel Investors: What Type Of Investor Am I?

There are many names for investors. Luckily, many of them mean the same things:

- **Seed investor**- this is a reference to where the company is in its lifecycle. A seed investor typically invests in business at the startup or beginning phase of the business.

- **Venture capitalist**- is an investor who provides capital to firms that exhibit high growth potential in exchange for an equity stake. This Investor is generally associated with a particular firm or fund.

- **Passive Investor**- an investor who does not participate in the day-to-day operations of the company (*there are other definitions as it relates to stocks or mutual funds*)

- **Active Investor**- an investor who takes a hands-on approach to investment. These types of investors are often involved in decision making, or in the day to day running of the business.

Accredited Versus Non-Accredited

Federal law defines those who can participate in certain types of investments. These rules are intended to ensure that the persons investing in an opportunity can accept the risks of loss, and are also able to remain financially stable afterwards.

The definition of an accredited investor is very specific. You are an accredited investor if:

•	Your earned income exceeds $200,000 (or $300,000 together with a spouse) in each of the two years prior, and is reasonably expected to remain the same for the current year,

OR

•	You have a net worth of over $1 million, either alone or together with a spouse (excluding the value of your primary residence).

An accredited investor could also be:

• Any trust, with total assets above $5 million, not formed specifically to purchase the subject securities, whose purchase is directed by a sophisticated person,

OR

• Any entity in which all of the equity owners are accredited investors.

If you fit into any of the above criteria, then you qualify as an accredited investor.

While there is no official place to register as an accredited investor, many companies or entities will have you self-declare that you meet the criteria. They may also request proof of your financial status.

A non-accredited investor is anyone who does not meet the criteria above. Most Americans fall into the non-accredited investor bucket.

Most accredited investors have many investment advice options, so I will be focusing on the non-accredited investor majority.

Venture Investment Or Main Street Investment

Venture investments include the flashy new technologies and gadgets that people associate with Silicon Valley. Think about the next Facebook or I-phone.

These businesses are called high growth companies, and are often associated with new and cutting-edge technology and/or business models.

These businesses can create multi-millionaires overnight but they are also very risky.

Predicting the wave of the future is more complicated than many think. It often takes more than 5 years to see these startups start to generate returns for their early investors.

Main street businesses, on the other hand, are the businesses that we utilize every day: restaurants, meat markets, fish markets, daycares, beauty supply stores, food trucks, hotels/motels, and the list goes on.

All of these businesses can generate outsized revenue, grow, and scale with the right amount of capital.

Angel investors can make a significant difference in these businesses as well. These businesses are revenue-generating and may be able to provide returns to their investors in as little as one month.

It is essential to know how you wish to make a difference as an investor.

Contrary to popular belief, venture investment and main street investment are of equal importance, and both can create economic power for its owners.

Understanding Your Role As An Angel Investor

Now that you understand some of the investment lingo as it relates to angel investing, let's talk about what your role as an angel investor will be.

The term 'Angel' came from the Broadway Theater when wealthy people were known to give money to theater companies to fund productions.

This might explain why most people believe that an angel investor's role begins and ends with signing and handing out large checks but it goes beyond that.

An Angel investor's role in a company goes beyond capital participation- Angel investors also add value to the business in diverse ways including but not limited to performance monitoring, coaching, providing sales leads, and overseeing the operations of the business.

As an Angel investor, you are probably a successful entrepreneur or a successful career man or woman yourself, and the knowledge and wealth of experience that you can bring to the business may even be more important than the cash.

A business with a lot of money to spend, but without a clear-cut strategy to utilize the funds optimally may still fail.

It's okay if you would prefer to play the role of a passive investor (because frankly, most angel investors rarely participate), but it is important to keep in mind that your returns are completely hinged on the success of the business – the more successful the business, the more profits you earn on your investment.

Studies have shown that businesses whose angel investors played active roles in the business are more likely to succeed than businesses whose investors simply signed the checks and took the back burner.

One study even showed that angel investors who interacted with their invested companies received at least three times more return than angel investors who did not.

As an Angel investor, you can play various roles in helping your invested business succeed. Let's take a look at five typical ways that you can participate in a business as an angel investor:

Coach/Mentor: Angel investors may also play the role of mentor or coach.

They may give regular advice or inputs that can help to move the business forward.

If you've spent years working in the Pharmaceutical industry for instance, and you're investing in a business that is also operating within the same industry, you would likely know more about how to navigate the waters compared to a set of newcomers.

The business can always take advantage of your connections, your experience, and your knowledge to move forward.

Sometimes, businesses have to hire the services of a consultant when charting unfamiliar territories and that would cost them a lot of money- what if you can step in and offer your services as a consultant and help the business save costs? This will go a long way in increasing the business's profit and invariably, your own returns.

Team Member: In addition to providing financial investment, you can also play a part-time role in the business such as serving on the board of directors, or serving in other capacities.

Reserve Force: You can be a passive investor who is also willing to help the entrepreneur on an as-needed basis. If the entrepreneur encounters some challenges, you can step in and help them solve the problem, or provide valuable insights that can help them navigate the waters.

Unofficial Marketer: This is one of the easiest extra roles that you can play as an Angel investor.

Every business craves more sales and revenue, and you can help your invested companies in this aspect by helping to spread the word about the business to your friends, family, to your network and groups you belong, or to your social media connections.

Financial Consultant: This is one aspect where a lot of entrepreneurs, especially startups, run into challenges.

I have seen startup founders with smart business ideas but zero idea on how to manage the financial aspects of their businesses, especially the working capital management and taxation aspects of their businesses.

While some larger or established businesses may be able to hire the services of professional Accountants or Tax Consultants to help them with the books, the mom-and-pop businesses and startups can do with some professional help and experience that comes free of charge.

These are only some of the typical ways that you can add value to your invested company as an Angel investor. In fact, this is one of the things that make the difference between an Angel and a Traditional Investor.

A Traditional Investor is only about his money- all he cares about is to see his investment portfolio double in size. He doesn't really care how the company does it, or how the business impacts the community.

But an angel is more of a humanitarian- you know that if this little business is able to thrive, a lot of people can benefit. The business can create employment for the unemployed, bring improvement to the community, and create generational wealth, so you don't just put in money; you contribute in whatever ways you can to drive the growth and success of the business.

Of course, you are not Santa Claus- your major goal is to make some profits but you do it bearing in mind that this business is more than just a money spinner.

Your participation will of course be subject to the disposition of the business owner. Some entrepreneurs may not be open to the idea of an investor participating in their businesses beyond capital provision. In that case, it's okay to take a backseat but you can just let them know how you can be of help, and that they shouldn't hesitate to reach out if they ever need help in those aspects of their business.

Investment Terms

While some terms are unique to venture investments, there are some common terms for both types of investments.

To help navigate which terms belong to which category, here is a quick color code:

Violet=Venture Investments

Blue=Main street Investments

Black= Both Types

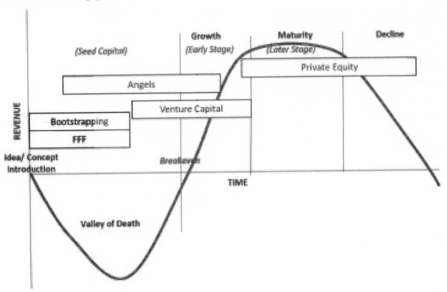

Company Stages

There are several stages of a startup:

Concept stage- This is also known as the idea stage.

At this stage, the startup has not solidified many key elements of the business, such as how the business will make money, who the target customers are, the product, and so on.

At this stage, a company is generally not ready for investors and should be self-funding or bootstrapping the concept.

This is not the stage for angel investors because this stage does not have enough "meat on the bones" to make an investment-wise.

Note: many new investors fall victim to the back of the napkin success story. While this has happened in history, it is not a very common story. Do not fall for quickly drawn ideas—save those investments for your billionaire years.

Pre-Seed- This stage is when a startup begins to test and validate the ideas that they decided on in the concept stage.

This could mean building a "proof of concept" to demonstrate the product, or conducting potential customer surveys to determine if they would be interested in the product or service.

I don't generally advise angels to invest at this stage unless the startup has a "prototype" built, and they have at least some indication of interest from potential consumers.

Seed- This stage is where the startup has a viable concept and is looking to gain traction.

This is where angel investors begin to appear. Angel capital may be used to complete the prototype or to aid in gaining early traction.

Early Stage- This stage is really where a company starts its journey.

At his stage the company has had its concept tested and vetted, and has refined the product based on the results. The product is ready to be introduced to the broader target market, and revenue *should* begin to be generated.

Angel investments are particularly critical at this stage because to generate revenue, several things need to be invested in, including marketing, inventory, and sales.

Growth and Mature Stage- These stages generally require more capital, and most angel investors don't have the money to contribute at this stage.

Note: If you decide to invest in established businesses within your community, they will likely be in the mature stage. These anchor businesses are the lifeblood of communities, and many would benefit from angels coming to their rescue.

The angel sweet spot for venture investment is in the pre-seed, seed, and early-stage phases of a business.

For main street investments, it is mostly the growth and mature stage; however, there may be opportunities to invest in a known market with a new location or concept moving into a new market.

The entrepreneurs may be new to business ownership and should be treated more like an unproven venture investment.

Marketing/Money Terms

Revenue- This is money generated from product sales.

This is different from profit. Profit is money left after all overhead and product or company costs are deducted. Most of the investments that angel investors make are not in companies that are generating profit.

Return on Investment (ROI) - Simply put, this is what you get back for your money.

If you are an investor, you are looking to make more than what you put in, and what you get as reward for your investments is called your Return on Investment (ROI).

Return is calculated in multiples. A 1x return means you got your money back, while 2x means you got double, 3X means you got three times what you invested, etc.

It's also possible to make negative returns known as a loss. This is often expressed in percentages, but the same math applies.

Convertible Notes- A convertible note is often used in the investment industry.

The funds from the Investor are treated as a loan, meaning the funds collect interest at a specified rate, and this interest is paid after an agreed period.

If the company cannot return the investment and the interest within the term of the note, then that note converts to ownership in the company, generally at a pre-determined conversion price.

Convertible notes allow the startup to get investments in without giving too much ownership early in the startup's life.

Convertible notes are a good option for investors as they allow funds to collect interest. They may also pay out at regular intervals, and offer the ability to gain ownership at a lower price.

Not all convertible notes have a voluntary conversion. This means that after a specified period, the Investor may gain ownership stake regardless of the payment.

Due Diligence- This involves investigating all the assumptions, and validating any statements that the company or business owner has made.

You should question everything that's presented. The more information you have, the more informed you can be about how your money would be used.

Valuation- This is what the company is worth.

Valuations at the early stages are often not very reliable especially if there is no revenue being generated, and the business has not received any other investments.

It is crucial to understand how the company reached its numbers and a valuation will give you an insight into what the company is truly worth.

Equity- This is the amount of ownership you receive in exchange for the investment, and this number may be a very small percentage.

It is unrealistic for an angel investor to expect equal (50%) or controlling (>50%) ownership. It is important to understand that requiring large stakes to be given at an early stage could inhibit the company from fundraising in the future, and that will inhibit the value of your stake.

Traction- This could come in two forms: money being generated from sales, or early customer acquisition.

I generally don't put much stock in traction that is free use or sign-up interest. This is because converting free customers to paid customers is not as easy a feat as most startups believe.

Exit- This is the time when the investor "cashes out" of an investment.

Exit events come in many different forms: cash outs, merger, bankruptcy, Initial Public Offering, Acquisition.

Scaling- simply stated, this means that a business is prepared to grow to a new level.

Growth has to be enabled. If a business generates more sales, but is unable to fill those orders or service all the new clients, the business could fail.

Growth requires planning, funding, systems and processes, proper staff levels, adequate technology, and sometimes, more partners.

Chapter Summary/Key Takeaways

In this chapter, we reviewed the basic terminology. While investment may require its own dictionary, the basics to know are: what kind of Investor am I, and how will I make my money back.

In the next chapter, you will be able to articulate this and pinpoint your angel characteristics.

CHAPTER TWO:
GETTING READY

I t goes without saying that if you are going to be an angel investor, you need money.

After reviewing the criteria for accredited versus non-accredited, you should be able to place yourself in a category. You should be able to decide what kind of investor you are, or can be.

Regardless of the group that you fit in, you need to assess where your finances currently are, and prepare your finances for investment.

How to Assess Where You Are

Personal Financial Audit

A personal financial audit can help decipher what your current financial status is. You'll be able to determine what your current net worth is, and most importantly, you'll be able to see areas where you can save costs so that you can afford to invest much quicker.

Conducting a personal financial audit sounds more technical and more painful than it is.

The best place to start is by looking at your current budget. Don't be embarrassed if you haven't been abiding by a budget. Start with the basics. How much money do you make per month? How much money do you spend?

A simple template is provided at the end of the chapter to help get you started.

To get a proper gauge, use 3-6 months of bank statements because using just one month or two can give a false impression of your spending habits.

Make notes of everything, no matter how small the purchase. Once you have a consistent number for what comes in and what goes out, start categorizing. The categories should be very descriptive; avoid, making broad bulk categories like miscellaneous or discretionary.

Once accurately categorized, separate all items into necessities/ essentials and non-necessities.

The essentials are:

1. Shelter (rent/mortgage)

2. Transportation (car payments, gas, bus/train passes, rideshare (if you have a car, do not include rideshare)

3. Food (groceries should be separated from takeout and restaurants).

4. Basic utilities (electricity, water, gas, basic internet).

5. Rainy day fund (savings are necessary to make sure that you don't need to call investments early).

The non-necessity category will have a lot more items. The first category should be debt. Debt should be broken into several categories:

1. Credit Cards

2. Personal loans or lines of credit

3. Student loans

4. Judgments or any other assessments, including taxes.

For many, this may be where most of your funds go.

Other categories will include shopping, restaurant, and bar tabs.

Paying off high-interest debts and resolving any judgments, is a must. While this may delay your initial investment plans, identifying areas where money is often wasted could help you redirect those funds into paying off your debts.

Once you have completed your financial audit, you can accurately assess where you are. The following scenarios will help you properly gauge where you are:

Scenario 1: If you have money left over each month, or have been able to identify areas where you can streamline your extra spending, you can begin accumulating those funds in a separate account.

Depending on what that amount is per month, you may be ready to invest in as little as 30-90 days.

Scenario 2: If you have high-interest debts and extra spending, you can pay down the highest interest debt with your other non-essential spending, and start your investor fund in 60-180 days.

This is highly dependent upon how aggressive you are with managing and paying off your debt.

Scenario 3: If you have high-interest debt and no extra spending, you will need to continue on a debt reduction pathway before investing. If you are in this scenario, you may need to wait 12 months before investing individually.

Take a very close look at non-essential areas where you can cut costs to increase your savings. For example, cable TV is an area where many people overlook. If you have already cut the cord but still subscribe to multiple streaming services, you may want to reduce those subscriptions too.

On average, most cord-cutters now pay for 3-4 streaming services. While individually, 7-15 dollars per month may not seem like much, but in 1 year, a single $15 account per month comes to $180. If you have four accounts, that's an extra $720 per year.

This is a small example; however, most budgets have these types of micro-savings that can add up.

Scenario 4: If you are spending more than you are bringing in, an effective spending reduction plan should be enacted before investing individually.

Each of the above scenarios assesses your unique capability to become an angel investor.

Investing Together

If you don't have a lot of money to spare right away, and you want to invest sooner- you don't want to wait for months or years to save up thousands of dollars, group economics may work better in your favor. Consider joining angel investment clubs or groups.

Angel investment clubs and groups are made up of a group of people who come together to contribute small amounts of money to invest collectively, and share the proceeds of the investments afterwards.

A group of 10 people contributing $500 once is a $5000 angel investment. Keep in mind; the goal is to begin investing, and not to focus so much on amassing large pools of money. For some businesses, $5000 in working capital investment can mean a new stream of revenue and return for your group.

We will discuss group dynamics and considerations in a later chapter.

So, How Much Do I Need To Get Started?

Whether together or individually, it is essential to decide how much you would like to invest.

I suggest having at least $2000 to invest for a start. While it is a small amount of capital, you will be able to identify potential opportunities accurately.

Personal Budgeting Template

Simple Budget			
How much money do you make per month? _____			
Item	Amount		
Salary/Pay			
Any additional Income			
Dividends			
Total			
How much do you spend per month? _____			
Item	Amount		
Bills			
Groceries			
Mortgage			
Credit cards			
Gas			

Laundry			
Car loan/payment			
Utilities			
Clothing			
Daycare			
Medical/Dental Insurance			
Savings			
Property taxes			
Other			
Total			
Income vs. Expenses			
Item	**Amount**		
Monthly income			
Monthly expenses			
Subtract the expenses from the income			

Chapter Summary/Key Takeaways

If you went through the steps in this chapter, then you should have determined three things.

- How much you have to invest

- How long until you have the pre-determined investment amount/ time to make your first investment

- Whether you will go forward individually or potentially with a group

In the next chapter, you will learn how to determine and find opportunities to invest in.

CHAPTER THREE: FINDING GOLD

The What

B efore you decide where to invest, you have to decide on what type of business interests you.
If you are working with a smaller investment budget, or simply looking to impact your community, then main street businesses may be the type of business you want to invest in.

These businesses are likely in staple industries like food/markets/restaurants, funeral homes, exterminators, car washes, flower shops, barbershops, or beauty salons.

Main street businesses may pose less risk to investors as they are already revenue-generating and have a consumer base. These types may be seeking capital to expand inventory, add a new product line, or renovate their properties.

If you are more interested in investing in new products or new ideas, then you should be looking at startups.

Startups are riskier investments but they often offer higher return potential compared to main street investments.

While many people worry about not having anything to invest in, in my experience, once the word gets out that you have money to invest (even if it's a small amount), you will be inundated with "opportunities".

There are lots of ways to identify potential investments but before you begin accepting and evaluating opportunities, it is essential to decide what you want to invest in.

How To Decide What To Invest In

I suggest making a list of the areas that you have expertise in, and your areas of interest. Never invest in things or industries that you don't know or understand no matter how hot the topic is, or what social media pundits are touting as the next big thing.

Expertise has very little to do with having learned something in school, or it being your job or career, your expertise may also come from personal experience.

For example, if you know hair salons based on your spending habits, or if you are a pet lover and have insights about pet products - that could be an excellent place to start.

While this may not strike you as expertise, you likely know more than you think about operations.

This is not to say that you should exclude topics that you studied in school, or ignore your career. I have found that investing is as much a science as it is an art. If you have both passion and experience, you may be able to develop what I call an 'investment gut.' Your investment gut will allow you to quickly decipher when something does not ring true, or when an opportunity just doesn't sound right.

Once you have narrowed your topics, then you can begin to look into external sources. These may include articles, news reports, or blogs that speak to trends within an industry.

If you decide to invest in something you don't know much about, you must educate yourself properly.

For example, many people find themselves interested in investing in real estate, cryptocurrency, or cannabis because of online chatter.

Many reality shows and influencers may give a false impression of how easy it is to earn a return. I have seen many people think that they can "flip" a house, or buy bitcoin and be millionaires in no time.

It is important to keep in mind that Investing is not a get rich quick scheme. If you are looking to invest in a trendy topic, you will need to spend considerable time in the preparation stage to make sure that you have a strong foundation about the market - where it has been and where it is going.

I suggest narrowing your initial investment interest to no more than two. Preferably, the interests should occupy the same industry category. Once you've gotten your bearings, you can now begin to diversify.

How To Seek Out The Right Investors

Seek, and You Shall Find

Now that we are all so interconnected- thanks to the internet- turning on your investor sign is easier than ever. However, a social media announcement may not be the best method for sourcing opportunities.

There are a number of smart ways to seek out investment opportunities with good potential.

Let's split investments into two buckets: main street businesses and startups.

Main Street Businesses

If you are seeking to make a more immediate impact in your community, invest in established businesses.

Here are a few ways to find good main street investment opportunities:

"A Place Where Everybody Knows Your Name."

Start with places you already patronize that align with your area of interest.

You can start some with basic surveillance- as a customer/ patron, look for ways in which your experience could be more enjoyable.

Do you love the product but dislike the service?

Are they always out of stock on your favorite item?

Would you love to stay inside the facility, but it's not very inviting?

Are there products that you consume that you wish you could buy and take home?

These are all areas of opportunities; opportunities that all require some capital investment.

Most mom-and-pop small businesses stay afloat but may not have the margins to cover payroll, overhead, and money to re-invest. Start by striking up a conversation with the owner, let them know about your observations.

Many owners have thought about the same improvements but lack the access to capital to make it happen whether through profit or loan from financial institutions.

If the owner is open to the discussion, let them know that you may be potentially interested in investing in the business. The owner's reply will be indicative of whether they are open to discussion or not.

Keep in mind that not all businesses want an investor or a partner, and it is not your job to convince them that it's a good idea.

A partner that is easy to work with will make your life easier, and give your investment the best opportunity to thrive.

If the answer is no, continue to patronize the business and keep building a relationship with the employees and the owners. Once a relationship has been established, then they may be more open to working with you.

Remember, build a relationship—once you have planted the idea of an investment, you don't have to bring it up again. A genuine relationship will get you farther.

"The Smoky Backrooms."

Business associations are a great way to learn about opportunities.

These associations may be trade groups, neighborhood coalitions, neighborhood business owner groups, or local chambers of commerce (especially the smaller affiliate chambers).

These groups host meetings and educational sessions that can bring many issues to the forefront. However, access to capital is a mainstay for many of these groups.

If you are unsure where to begin, then start with a specific program or activity. I suggest a program that is focused on access to capital. That way, you know that you are in the room with lots of people who are seeking investment.

Another way to get a full lay of the land is to volunteer.

By volunteering, you are building a relationship with the group, and this will give you first-hand knowledge of the neighborhood- *and the neighbors are always chatting.*

When in these rooms, don't be shy about introducing yourself as someone interested in investing in the community. Those that are interested will follow-up.

There is no need to rush to sign-up for full membership of any of these groups; try out the group well before you make a membership investment.

"Your Friendly Neighborhood Banker."

If you have not already done so as a part of your financial audit when opening your investment account, then meet with your banker.

Small business bankers are well-tuned into the community.

I always recommend having an account with a community bank or a credit union. These banks are generally more intimately ingrained into the community as opposed to their big-box counterparts.

They see businesses of all stripes and levels seeking capital via loans or lines of credit, often having to deny them, or turn them away because they don't meet the lending criteria.

While they will not be able to give you customer details, you can provide them with the leeway to share your information or introduce such customers.

Higher Education

In recent years, the Small Business Administration (SBA) has partnered with local colleges or Universities to create Small Business Development Centers (SBDC's).

These centers were established to provide business-related assistance and knowledge to help entrepreneurs start, run, and grow their businesses. These services are often offered at a low cost or free of charge.

While they act as a tremendous resource, they often lack the capital to help many businesses with needs that extend beyond education or programming.

Across the United States and Puerto Rico, there are nearly 1,000 SBDC's.

Find one close to you and make an appointment with one of the center's representatives. Tell them what you are looking to invest in. They will likely know of many businesses that need capital.

Startups

A startup is a new business that is less than five years old by most definitions.

According to the SBA, over 627,000 businesses are started each year so you will have no problems finding investment opportunities.

Research shows that startups in accounting, online retail, construction, and landscaping were most likely to get started with under $5,000 in startup costs (Trends, n.d.).

However, if you are going to invest in startups, I suggest having at least $10,000 in capital.

This may seem like a lot of savings; however, if after your financial audit you were able to save $27.40 every day for one year, you will have $10,000 individually to invest.

This number is reduced if you are a part of a collective group; an investment group of 30 with each member investing $822 will get the group to $10,000 quickly.

In addition to the suggestions above, there are several avenues for identifying startup investment opportunities.

Crowdfunding

Crowdfund raisers help startups reach their capital goals by collecting small amounts from large groups.

There are two types of crowdfunding campaigns- those that raise equity, and those that give in-kind products or promotional items in exchange for investments.

You should only consider those campaigns raising equity if you want a financial return.

Crowdfunding campaigns are usually hosted on platforms that are regulated, and the terms of the deal are pre-determined.

Often, these campaigns are for startups with technology components, but they represent many industries.

Depending on the campaign, minimum contributions can be as low as $100.

Pitch Competitions

A lot of startups turn to pitch competitions to raise capital and hone their pitching skills.

Many of these competitions are open to the public, and allow you to hear about the companies and hear the expert judges.

While there will be a winner announced, that doesn't necessarily mean that it is the best company, so feel free to reach out to whichever concept or founders most resonate with you.

To right-size the best potential investment, choose competitions with prizes that are similar to your investment size.

Business or Technology Conferences

These are conferences are typically aimed at new startups.

While the program itself may not particularly be of interest to you, the demonstration day or the exhibitor space should be.

Attending or participating in these components of the conference is usually free, and allows the startup to set up a booth and interact with the public. This is your opportunity to meet founders and discuss potential investment opportunities.

Social Media

Social media is by far, my least favorite way of discovering an investment opportunity. However, many people are more comfortable in cyberspace.

I do not recommend that you create a post saying you have money that you want to invest for many reasons.

Here are my suggested tips for finding opportunities via social media:

In the headline portion of your social media page, describe yourself as an investor, and define the industry you are interested in.

Those looking for investors will find you as they search for specific profile descriptors. This method works best on LinkedIn, Instagram, and Twitter.

Be careful with opening random links and attachments on social media, and avoid giving out any personal information.

Chapter Summary/Key Takeaways

There are many opportunities to get involved as an investor. In this chapter, we discuss many novel ways to find investment opportunities.

Some other considerations before you start your search:

- Create a separate email account that is dedicated to sending and receiving investment information.

- Pull in several opportunities; don't let your investment money burn a hole in your pocket.

Many venture capital firms see more than 1000 opportunities in a year. Cast your net wide.

- Stick to the area that you decided to invest in. Don't get distracted by other opportunities that are off base.

- While you are looking for opportunities, keep your funds separate and continue to build the account as you are gathering information.

If you have created a strong relationship with your banker, they will have likely set you up with an account that collects some interest. Even if a small amount- it is usually worth it.

Do not have an ATM card issued on the account and do not connect it to your other accounts.

Remember, learning about the opportunities is not a second job but an enjoyable experience.

If you have chosen an area that you enjoy, you will be able to learn more about the industry.

Focus on building a relationship, and the opportunities will be endless.

PART II: THE MORE YOU KNOW

"Risk comes from not knowing what you are doing"

-Warren Buffet

In this section we will discuss how to evaluate potential opportunities. We will discuss:

- How to Vet a Business or Idea Before You Invest
- Preparing for due diligence
- Which documents to request
- Holistic evaluation
- Setting expectations
- A making a selection
- Deciding how much return is acceptable

CHAPTER FOUR:
DEEP DIVE PREP

In my experience, the diving line between a lousy investment and a smart one is the amount of due diligence that is conducted before investing. While diligence does not guarantee you a return, it does equip you with information that will help you make a wise decision.

Remember, due diligence is merely an investigation process. At this stage, you have to think of yourself as an investment detective.

When seeking investors, every business will show you its best qualities. You will likely only hear about the upside and how great things are going. It becomes up to you to find the warts, expose the weaknesses, and identify the risks and other points of failure.

I have seen individual investors and large corporations overpay, or take heavy losses because the information they were given were not verified.

Many investors shy away from the diligence process for two main reasons; they don't want to seem pushy, or they have a phobia for the math and numbers.

As it relates to being pushy, it is your money, and there is no need to be a jerk, but there is also no need to be seen as the nicest person on earth.

Remember, you're an angel now—and you are here to help, but you have to be sure that you are helping in the right way.

For those with a number's repulsion, a fundamental rule to keep in mind is that the numbers should be simple and easy to understand.

It is the business's responsibility to explain them and breakdown how they arrived at a number. If it doesn't make sense, it isn't on you to figure it out.

Others make mistakes in thinking that because they are intelligent, they are experts at everything.

Being an expert or being successful in one area of business does not guarantee you success in another. Every industry has its nuisances and norms, especially if the industry is undergoing a paradigm shift.

Apply what you know but make sure not to drink your own Kool-Aid.

And some believe that they can just "read" people and tell if something is a good investment. I am a big believer in trusting your gut, but you are not a psychic or a mind reader.

I have seen lots of smart people and "instinct" driven people being taken advantage of- a scammer can see you coming from a mile away.

It is therefore necessary to have a strong diligence protocol in place, and it is easy to create one and replicate the process every time you need to investigate a business you're looking to invest in.

In this chapter, we will break down the process into small bits.

A key factor to keep in mind is that you are not going to conduct a deep dive due diligence on every opportunity. You only need to do this with businesses that you are excited about.

If you are indifferent, or just mildly interested in hearing more, it is not worth your time.

Also, avoid initiating a diligence process if you are not serious about writing a check. It is not fair to the businesses, and you do not want to gain a reputation as a person who is just kicking the tires. Word will spread fast and people may start finding it hard to take you serious.

Let's get ready to take the deep dive.

Proceed With Caution: How to Vet a Business Idea

In your search for viable businesses to invest in, you'll likely find a lot of businesses that seem like they may need some financial help or need saving but before you even begin to consider investing in any business, you have to first vet the business and if it's a startup, you have to vet the idea.

This helps you sieve the wheat from the chaff and ensure that you are giving your money to people who have similar interests- people who are looking to grow their businesses and make a difference in the community not just people looking to cash out, or people who may end up wasting your money.

One tool that Angel investors and Venture Capitalists use to sieve the wheat from the chaff is the **Business Plan**.

In this day and age, every serious entrepreneur should have a business plan.

There is a common saying that until you write something down, it's only a wish.

It only becomes a plan after you have written it down.

A business plan is a document that outlines the goals of a business, and how it plans to achieve those goals.

Business ideas are a dime a dozen- anyone can dream up ideas but turning ideas into profit requires a plan.

During your search, you'll come across a lot of sweet-talking entrepreneurs with tall dreams and no concrete strategies for achieving those dreams.

Like I said earlier, you're not Santa Claus- you're looking to make money while impacting your community, and that means that you cannot afford to put your money in places where it won't make a difference.

This is why you must always, always ask for a business plan whether the business is a small mom-and-pop corner shop, or a startup. Every business should have that simple document that clearly details:

- Who they are

- What they do

- Where they've been

- Where they are going

- Why they need more money

- How they plan to spend it

Basically, the business plan should detail how the money you give them will make a difference, or help them reach their goals.

A business plan can be one of the earliest ways to tell a viable investment from a disaster waiting to happen.

After meeting with a business owner and establishing that they are open to the idea of an angel investor, ask them for a business plan and study it carefully before you decide to go further with them.

The business plan doesn't have to be formal, or be in the standard format because many small business owners may not know how to prepare one, and may not be able to afford the services of an expert but there are a few standard questions that every business plan should be able to provide answers to, and every serious entrepreneur should have these answers in their head.

For business owners who are unable to prepare a standard business plan, you can arrange a meeting with them, ask them the necessary questions, and help them write it down.

A business plan should be able to answer the following questions:

- **What is Your Basic Business Concept?** This is where you learn what the business is truly about- the product or services they offer, business locations, and other basic introductory information about the business.

- **What is Your Goal?** This is almost the same the same thing as asking a potential employee the *"Where do you see yourself in the next 10 years"* question in order to see if they fit into your company.

Remember, you're looking to invest in businesses with sustainable growth and development plans for the future, businesses that can be passed down from one generation to another, not businesses that may collapse within a few years.

- **How Do You Plan to Implement It?** This is another area you want to pay close attention to.

For every goal, the business owner must have a clear and sensible plan to achieve it. Keep in mind that your money is going into those goals so you have to be sure that the business owner knows what they are doing, and isn't just trying to build castles in the air.

- **What Competitive Advantage Do You Have Over Your Competitors?** This is especially important when trying to invest in Main street businesses. Many main street businesses operate in industries that are oversaturated and with low barriers for entry.

If you want to invest in such businesses, you have to be sure that it can stand out from the others, or that they have a trick up its sleeves for gaining competitive advantage over others.

- **Who are Your Target Customers?** If the business is seeking to enter a new market, find out who the customers are to see if any opportunities exist in the market they are looking to enter.

- **How Do You Plan to Reach Them?** This is where you ascertain that the company has concrete plans for reaching its target customers. You want to look at things like distribution channels, marketing, and advertising strategies.

- **Who would be managing the Business?** A business is only as good as its managers, and when I say managers, I'm talking about the employees too.

In a business, everybody who is involved in the day to day operations of the business is also a manager. Every single individual contributes significantly to the success or failure of the business whether it's the security guard manning the doors, the waitresses taking and serving orders, or the manager who plans everything on paper.

You can have all the fancy ideas in the world but if you don't have the right hands and minds to help you implement those ideas, the business may still fail.

So, you want to be sure that the businesses you invest in have capable managers and employees that can help to make the business owner's dream come true.

And if it's a typical sole-proprietorship with no employees, study the personality of the owner closely, and be sure that they have what it takes to achieve the goals that they have outlined.

- **How Much Do You Need and How Do You Plan to Spend It**: Every business owner seeking capital investment must have an expense budget detailing the total amount they need, and how they plan to spend it.

This is another tool you can use to gauge the viability of the investment. You'll be able to see what they plan to do with your money, if their plans are necessary or relevant to their goals, and if their sales and earnings projections are sufficient to recoup the expenses and earn you any returns or profits within your planned investment period.

For example, if you are looking to invest for 2 years, you want to be sure that the company is able to company can make enough profits to recoup your investments with interests within 2 years.

If an entrepreneur tells you they need $40,000 for instance, and you are only looking to invest for one year, whereas the company only makes $2000 in monthly profits at the moment and have projected that your investment will help them increase that to $4,000 a month, it means they won't be able to refund your money let alone give you any interests on your investments within one year.

Because even if they handed all of their profits to you (which is very unlikely), it will take at least ten months to recoup your investments before even talking about the interests.

So, these are areas you want to look closely into:

How much does the business need?

How much are they currently making?

What is the minimum length of time it will talk them to recoup the money I give them together with interests?

Can I wait for that long?

You should only consider investing when you have looked into these parameters and you are satisfied with the results.

By requesting a business plan, you are not only protecting your interests, you are also doing the business owner a favor.

A business plan can serve as a blueprint for growth that the owner can always refer back to in the future. It's like having a GPS installed in your vehicle- you know where you are going, where you don't want to go, and how you can get to your destination without unnecessary detours and distractions.

Also, like the saying goes, two good heads are better than one. While looking at the business plan, you may also be able to come up with valuable insights and ideas that the business owner might not have even thought about.

And even if you don't end up investing with them, they can still gain a lot from the advice you give.

So now, you've seen the business plan and you're interested in investing in the business- what next?

Well, you still have to investigate the business further by doing due diligence.

This is the stage where you tell the business owner to provide documents and proofs to back up everything they've told you so far.

Before You Dive In

Just like putting the funds together to invest took some building work, the due diligence process is going to require some organizing.

Before you begin your review, you need to pull in a critical team member, an attorney.

Everyone should have a relationship with an attorney, specifically, an attorney that specializes in business transactions.

There are some essential documents or agreements that you will need to have your attorney prepare and review: A non-disclosure agreement, a term-sheet, an agreement, and an exit/ release agreement.

Non-disclosure Agreement

A Non-disclosure agreement is also known as a confidentiality agreement. This agreement is needed to protect the information that is shared by both parties.

As an investor, you want to do everything you can to ensure that the businesses you wish to invest in feels protected with you.

You will be asking for lots of sensitive data, and in the black community, money matters are an especially sensitive area.

I recommend a two-way or mutual NDA.

You may also need to disclose information to the business owner or, you may want your identity as an investor protected.

One key clause to pay close attention to is the terms of the agreement.

In an initial NDA, you will not need more than 18 months in an agreement. The longer the term, the longer you will be on the hook for maintaining those documents.

Choose terms that are suitable for the length of time you are investigating. An extended period can be included in the full investment agreement should you get there.

Term Sheet

This can be a very simple document outlining what you are offering, and what you expect in return.

There are some key components to be included:

- How much you are investing, when, and how.

Some investors prefer to invest in increments, although this will not be relevant for smaller dollar amounts.

Be sure to place achievable disbursement dates as the business may be depending on those funds.

- What you expect in return and when.

If you are expecting interest payments, then be sure to outline when those payments start, and how often they are to be made.

If you are to receive a percentage of ownership, it is important to outline how that will be paid.

Are you expecting a set percentage of the monthly/quarterly/annual revenue?

In my experience, it is crucial to hammer these things out in the term sheet rather than wasting time with a full agreement.

An Agreement

This is the full agreement. This has all terms from the term sheet, as well as the legal protections in the event that there is a failure to abide with the agreed-upon terms.

This will tell both parties how to solve a problem, and when it's time to pull that trigger.

An Exit/Release

Some investments are for a shorter amount of time. It is important to place something in writing that says your obligation has been fulfilled, and both parties are released from the agreement.

Why Use an Attorney?

In this day and age, there are lots of information on the internet that can give an investor a false sense of security.

Some investors may decide that since there are a lot of legal forms and templates for contractual agreements on the internet, they don't need to hire a lawyer to draft one for them.

But you may expose yourself to a lot of risks when you pull a document off the internet and use it, especially when it has to do with investment contracts and agreements.

There is no such thing as a standard contract- there are details that will be important for different deals, or that will vary from industry to industry.

Some legal platforms offer legal documents at low-costs. Semi-customization is always better than pulling a document off the internet, but it's still a risky prospect. Depending on the platform, and the contents of the document, the legal documents may still pose a risk.

Many people shy away from using an attorney due to the fear of the costs; however, attorneys are always less expensive on the front end of a partnership as opposed to when you have to bring them in after the situation has gone bad.

Nonetheless, there are a few cost-saving measures that you can deploy to keep your costs low.

If you do not have a trusted attorney in your life already (or one that is connected to a firm that offers representation in multiple areas), then you can meet with several attorneys and see what their capabilities and hourly rates are.

Be upfront with the attorney, and let them know that you are looking for counsel and looking to make the right decision.

Do not string them along or promise your business just to see how they might operate. They are most effective when you are honest.

In the conversation, do pay attention to how the attorney interacts with you. If they make you feel dumb, or you do not understand what they are talking about, or they seem annoyed by questions, then they are not the attorney for you.

Think of your attorney like your priest- you have to be comfortable with them because you will need to tell them everything.

To save attorney costs, you can try one or more of the following methods:

Bundling

Bundling is exactly what it sounds like. Some attorneys offer packages of documents for a set price. They likely have worked with lots of businesses with similar needs so they have designed go-to packages.

Some attorney's also offer prepaid hour packages. These packages generally come with some discount on the hourly rate if you prepay for pockets of time.

Not all firms offer these options, but it never hurts to ask.

Review Only

If you are particularly sensitive to pricing, and you are comfortable writing, then you may want to consider writing out your documents and having an attorney review them to ensure they offer adequate protection.

Skip the formalities or trying to sound like an attorney, and stick to regular language. Write exactly what you mean.

A simple straight forward agreement will get you significantly farther than trying to be fancy.

Opp

That's right- Other People's Property.

You can save on some costs by requesting to execute the other person's agreement, but I still suggest having an attorney review it so that you know what is in the agreement.

Remember, generally, the person who creates the document will make sure that it favors their position. If you decide to use documents provided for you-YOU MUST READ THEM THOROUGHLY!

Start-Up Investing

If you are more interested in investing in startups rather than main street businesses, the need for legal review and representation is heightened as you are much more likely to need to protect the proprietary information of a startup.

The term sheet and ultimately, the agreement or convertible note, will not be a simple two-page agreement. It most likely will be 5+ pages in length.

While you can deploy some of the strategies mentioned above, including having an attorney read and review the documents provided to you, it is not recommended that you do this alone.

Having an attorney can be very helpful in negotiations and re-solving disputes without going to court.

No matter what avenue you decide, do not simply skip putting things in writing. Handshake deals are a terrible deal and usually come back to bite you.

Remember, everyone hears conversations differently, so it is essential to get things in writing, so everyone is on the same page.

Chapter Summary/Key Takeaways

In this chapter, we discuss the importance of due diligence and having the proper documentation, and how to go about it without burning a hole in your pocket or exposing yourself to avoidable risks.

An attorney can be critical to protecting you.

However, when just starting out cost savings can be a major consideration hence, we have discussed several options that can reduce your cost burden, but still provide you with the necessary protection.

In the next chapter, we discuss how to move into due diligence: which documents to request, and what to look for.

CHAPTER FIVE: PROVE IT!

As we discussed previously, the due diligence process is that part of the investment process where you are telling the business to prove that what they are saying is true. You should always verify everything, especially those details that are most crucial to your decision making.

Before you begin requesting information, be sure to sign a non-disclosure agreement first.

The Laundry List

Each section outlines documents to request. In each section, there will be documents that are non-negotiable and a necessity, and some that may not be necessary depending on the stage of development the business is currently in, or the industry in which they operate.

Corporate Documents

1. **Articles of Incorporation**- The articles of incorporation are a must-have document whether the business is a startup or a main street business.

This document tells you that the business is registered with the Secretary of State.

If you are looking into a main street business or a startup with a brick and mortar location, then the business should be incorporated in the state where the site is, or be appropriately registered as an out of state entity that has permission to operate in the state.

If the business is a startup that is tech-based or tech-enabled, then the company's articles of incorporation may be in another state.

Delaware, for instance, is a popular state of incorporation.

Even if the company provides you with a PDF file of the articles of incorporation, be sure to go to the website of the secretary of state for that state, and look up the entity.

Be sure that the company is still current in the database.

Also, verify who the registered owner of the business truly is just to be sure that you are negotiating with the right person.

In main street businesses, it is not uncommon for a parent to be the actual owner of a business, and the children to have taken over.

However, if you see that the business changes owners frequently or the company has been administratively dissolved, you should make a note, and ask follow-up questions. Frequent owner changes could signal financial or legal issues, and administrative dissolution may be revealing some documentation deficits that should be explored.

The business will need to be properly registered before you move forward with the investment.

Depending on the industry, there may be other registration requirements.

2. **Bylaws, Operating, Partnership Agreements**- An operating agreement, and/or bylaws, should be present

if you are considering a startup.

Main street businesses may not have taken this step, especially if there is only one owner.

The operating/ partnership agreements include the rules of the business functioning. If there are multiple members of the company, how decisions, including investment decisions are to be made, are spelt out in the operating/partnership agreements.

It's always good to know who has the final say in the company, and to familiarize yourself with what your potential role may be as outlined in the document.

3. **Certificates from All States and Jurisdictions where the Company Does Business**- This is similar to the articles of incorporation.

Every state that the business operates in should be appropriately accounted for and documented.

4. *Other Ownership Agreements- Request any other agreements that grant ownership stakes to others.*

For a main street business, this could be another investor, and for a startup, this could be other outstanding convertible notes.

If they do exist, you will need to factor that into your decision.

First, do some quick math. Be sure to make that the ownership stake being offered is available.

I have seen cash strapped owners offer portions of their business to multiple people, and end up giving away more than 100%.

If the startup has other outstanding convertible notes, pay close attention to the amount of interest that they are currently paying.

Convertible notes are a great option, but they can saddle a startup with burdensome payments early in their revenue-generating life.

Financial Information

The financial information should be a core focus of your diligence.

Every business should have a handle on their finances if they are a viable investment prospect. Having a handle on your finances means knowing how much money you bring in each month, and how much you spend.

The business should have some established system for tracking this information.

For established businesses, this may be a point-of-sale system tracking the register or credit card systems.

Cash-only businesses are a bit harder to verify. For this reason, investing in a cash-only business may be risky.

Startups that are pre-revenue may have limited financials. They are more likely to have forecasts but not sales records.

1. **Official Financial Statements**- For main street businesses, this will likely be tax returns.

It is important to request several years, 3-5 years.

It is important to look for trends: Are the sales growing or are they flat? Does the business show a profit?

Be sure to compare the tax returns to any internal accounting documents. If you see discrepancies between what is reported to the IRS, and what the owner says to you, this is a red flag.

The last thing you want is the IRS coming into the picture and auditing the business that you just took a stake in.

While it is positive for the company have a professional independently preparing the financials, do not penalize the company if they don't, especially if the books are in good order.

> 2. **Budget**- The business should have a profit and loss statement.

They may not call it a P&L, but the business should know what it brings in, and what it spends. This is not negotiable.

> 3. **Financial Projections**-Financial projections are a must for a startup.

A poorly kept secret is that in general, financial projections are not very reliable.

The projections for a startup should be for five years but pay more attention to the projections for years 1 to 3.

Projections are based on assumptions or the startup's best hypothesis on what will happen. These assumptions should be very clear.

They include how many customers they will sell to each year, how much they will charge, how much the product or service will cost the business, employee salaries, etcetera.

Pay close attention to a few key factors. If the sales go from 0 to 1 million in the first year, the projections are likely worthless. Sales take time to develop, so it is unlikely that a 7-figure business will emerge in year one.

Pay attention to how many employees, especially sales employees. A mistake several new startups make is projecting sales with no employees.

A single founder will be wearing a lot of hats, and if they are the only person driving sales, their sales are likely to fall short of their projections.

Finally, look at the profit margin, including taxes. Most startups do not turn a profit in the first few years. If the company is projecting a profit, take a look at whether they have accounted for taxes.

If they have not, then it is likely that they missed other costs.

It is vital to question the projections but do keep in mind that this is an area most entrepreneurs get wrong.

Use your own analysis to adjust the projections.

4. **Current Business Plan**- Every business should have some sort of plan for the future.

If the business is a main street, this is likely to be much less formal. Often, an owner will have the plan in their head.

If this is the case, you need to listen carefully and document the plan in a quick and easy way.

If they have been looking to expand offerings, or do renovations, they should have some costs that correspond to their plans.

All startups should have a more formalized business plan. Expect these plans to include robust sales and marketing strategy, and a technology or platform development plan.

Competitive intelligence, complete financials, and market data should be thorough.

5. **Accounts Receivable and Accounts Payable**- This only applies to the established main street businesses and startups that are generating revenue.

Accounts receivable are the amounts owed to a company by its customers, while accounts payable are the amounts that a company owes to its suppliers.

Be sure to pay close attention to both line items.

If there are a lot of accounts receivable dollars that have been outstanding for greater than 90 days, that is a potential red flag that the company is carrying significant bad debt.

In other words, they are making sales, but the customers are not paying on time.

If there are lots of payable dollars outstanding, that could indicate cash flow problems or possibly bad credit with suppliers.

The business should also disclose if it has write-offs/bad debt.

6. **Product or Service Pricing Plans and Policies**-No matter the type of business it is, there should be defined pricing.

This may, or may not be a stand-alone document.

When evaluating the pricing structure, think about it from the perspective of a customer.

Make sure that the pricing makes sense for the customer base.

If the company is a startup, there should be some data (a survey, industry trends, or competitor pricing) that gives some guidance.

7. **Contracts and Agreements**- All agreements or contracts should be in writing.

If there are large (major corporate) agreements, it is important to review those documents.

Specifically, you should figure out how long is left on the contract, and verify that they are in good standing.

If there is a new contract, like a new government contract for example, be sure that you understand what is needed to secure the contract fully, and when the first payments will come in.

Be careful with "partnerships" that do not yield actual revenue. While some partnership can boost credibility, investigate and determine whether that increase in credibility has yielded any results.

If there is no documentation of the agreement, do not use it as a factor for investment.

8. **Who They Owe**- If the company owes anyone money, be sure to know the necessary details.

You should know how much is owed, what the monthly payments are, and whether the company is current or in default.

Be sure to ask about liens, equipment leases, mortgages, or any other outstanding loans or debt that reduces the company profit.

Compliance

This will vary significantly from business to business.

One common compliance document is business insurance. Every business has risks, and insurance helps to reduce that risk should things go wrong.

Certain industries require specific limits, so be sure that the business is in compliance.

All permits and licenses should be verified to be current and in good standing.

Litigation

Conduct a public record - check to be sure that no legal cases are outstanding.

If your search finds a case, then fully understand the status, including potential damages.

Search for any other claims or public filings like bankruptcy or liens on any property.

If any cases have been settled, be sure that it has been properly documented, and the business has fulfilled its part of the bargain.

Management And Personnel

For main street businesses, the employees who manage and interact with customers are critical.

Don't be surprised if the owner has hired several family members. This can be both a blessing and a curse.

Hiring family can mean increased loyalty, but it can also mean lax enforcement of business rules and procedures.

Observe family dynamics in the business settings to understand the potential risks.

If the company is a startup, the management should be a particular focus. If the startup has only one team member-the founder, that is a potential red flag.

Everyone needs a team.

Understand the background of the founder. Do they have industry experience? If the answer is no, then the need for a team is of greater importance.

Do not mistake education for experience. Education does confer some knowledge but it is not a substitute for hands-on experience. Both are important but don't count a business owner or founder out because they do not have a formal education.

Pay close attention to the organizational management chart and bios of senior personnel. Even the savviest investors place great importance on the quality of the management team.

Intellectual Property

This will not apply to all companies or startups.

Intellectual property includes Patents, trademarks, and trade secrets. Having intellectual property can give a competitive advantage.

If the company has a recognizable brand, a trademark is important.

If the company has trade secrets, these should remain secret. These will not, and should not be disclosed to you. Trade secrets only keep their value if few people know it.

Finally, patents are great but very expensive to secure and maintain, and typically take years to acquire.

Some terms to listen for are patent-pending, filed, granted, and abandoned.

A filed patent means just that. It means that the paperwork is on record at the patent office.

Patent-pending means that the patent is moving through the system.

An abandoned patent means that the process was started, but the business did not follow it through.

It is important to note that even though abandoned patents can be revived, the process is not as simple as filing again on the same product.

Granted patents are the most valuable. These give the most protection.

However, pay attention to how much time is left before it expires.

Twenty years is the usual term of a patent, and having much time left is very important.

Also, note that intellectual property is a very complex field. If the founder or owner filed the application, it might have a more difficult time getting through.

Use Of Funds

Simply put, this is how the business intends to use your investment.

This should be clear, with the numbers well defined.

Large buckets like working capital or sales growth are not sufficient. Those are headers- there should be more details on the line items.

The costs should also be verifiable. While the funds may be coming in the nick of time, make sure that they are enough to weather the storm. If the funds only help for a month or two before the business is back in a rut, then this may not be a wise investment.

Two final keys to diligence are the interview, and the visit(s).

You should have extended conversations with the owners.

You should never refer to the interactions as interviews, but you will use them as assessments, much like a job interview, to gain insights into the owner's mindset and personality.

Visit or patronize the business several times. If there is a physical brick and mortar establishment, allow the owners to give you a formal tour and after that, visit the business unannounced a few different times.

You should observe the business when customer traffic is high, and when it is at the lowest.

If the target is a startup, then go through the business' process.

If it is a service, go through the process as an unannounced or secret shopper. But first, have a good understanding of how the founder has described the process before you visit. Your secret shopper experience should give you an insight into what other customers are receiving.

In both of these scenarios, be sure that you are not receiving any preferential treatment. It may be necessary to send an associate so that you are not recognized.

Chapter Summary/Key Takeaways

Remember that the diligence process is your opportunity to verify all that has been presented to you. No company is perfect, and there may be gaps in the documentation.

Do not be shy when requesting documents. If the owner or the founder is irritated with the requests for documentation, walk away.

The diligence process is not intended to cause embarrassment or harm.

Pay close attention to whether the documents match the narrative. Trust is a key component of any investment. If the owner is continuously correcting the record or has complicated explanations, this is not a positive sign and should not be ignored.

Careful investigation on the front end of any investment will save you pain, time, and money.

In the next chapter, you will learn about setting expectations and how to evaluate the opportunity and all of the documents as a whole.

CHAPTER SIX:
KNOWING WHEN

I n the previous chapter, we discuss documents to request when considering investing.
Unless you have been an attorney, or in a finance position, you may be saying great, I have all of this information, now what?

How do I move through these documents, and make sense of them?

There are plenty of resources that can teach you how to read a profit and loss statement or how to make sense of a marketing strategy, but I will instead walk you through scenarios.

Like Kenny Rogers famously wrote: ...*You've got to know when to hold 'em, know when to fold 'em, know when to walk away, and know when to run...*

Like the gambler, an investor has to know when to go all the way in, and when to run away.

Know When To Hold 'Em

These are your best-case scenarios- the opportunities to hold on to and make an investment.

Scenario 1

In this scenario, the company has all of its documents in good order and is current.

This is not a likely scenario as angel investors are needed by those who are bootstrapping their way through and in need of some assistance.

If you are looking for a business that has all green lights and no red flags, then you will likely never invest a single dollar.

Scenario 2

The Shiny Parts:

- You have met with the owners of the business and have a rapport. They are open to your ideas, and you are comfortable with their vision of how to grow.

- The owners are financially vested in the business. This means the business should be the primary source of income of its owner.

As a first-time investor, you want to be sure that the owner will take the wins and losses with you.

- The business has been in the area for more than five years, is seen as a staple, and enjoys a good reputation.

- The business is properly registered, and all insurance and business permits are in place.

- The business is generating revenue and clears at least a small profit.

- The business is not carrying any substantial debt and has not defaulted on their loan obligations. The business may have a mortgage, but it is current, and there are no second or third mortgages.

The Warts:

- The business's profit is minimal—they may have thin margins for their industry, or the slim profit margins may be due to poor purchasing power, incorrect pricing, or top-heavy human resource burdens.

- The business has some amount of "downtime" or low customer traffic a few days of the week.

- The building/facility could use some improvements- either aesthetic or structural.

- Little to no marketing outside of word of mouth or local legend.

A company in this scenario may make a good investment as this company has good financial health.

All of the warts mentioned above are all areas where your capital can be used to make a difference.

The most attractive of all the shiny parts (in addition to being profitable), is the owner's coachability. This serves as a foundation for a good investment relationship.

This scenario is more likely to be a main street business because very few early-stage startups are likely to be generating any revenue or profit.

Know When To Fold 'Em

The scenarios in this category cover those investments that are going to require a bit of work before you are all in.

Scenario 1

The Shiny Parts:

- The owners have a clear vision of how to grow the business.

- The owners may be financially vested in the business.

This could be a second or third business, so they have some sort of business track record.

- The business owner enjoys a good reputation, or has credibility in the industry and/or in the community.

- The business is properly registered, and all insurance and business permits are in place.

- The business is generating revenue.

- The business is carrying some debt, and the debt may be eating profit margin, but they are current on all debt obligations.

The Warts:

- The business has no profit— while the business is making money, the overhead is destroying the margins.

- There is a significant amount of operational inefficiency.

- The business has a large amount of "downtime" or low customer traffic throughout the week. There may be only one or two days that actually support the business.

- The building/facility could use some improvements- either aesthetic or structural.

- Little to no marketing outside of word of mouth, or local legend.

Scenario 2

- The owner wants to grow but does not have a defined vision for how that will happen.

- The business has been in the area for more than one year and is on an upswing for customer traffic and growth.

- The business is properly registered, and all insurance and business permits are in place.

- The business is generating some revenue but is currently operating at a loss.

The Warts:

- The business is carrying substantial debt but is current.

- The business is operating at a loss due to the debt burden or overhead.

- Poor foot traffic due to the young age of the business.

- The building/facility is newer but not owned.

- There is some marketing, but it is still too soon to tell if it is effective and will generate repeat business.

The investments in this category may still be a quality one, but it will require a bit more of a hands-on approach.

You will need to help develop a plan and strategy, and you may also need to help out with the execution.

If these are not your strong suits, always use the Hippocratic Oath approach—first, do no harm.

You want to come in as a help, not another burden.

In these scenarios, if you will have to contribute your talent and expertise in a significant way, you can negotiate a higher ownership stake.

Know When To Walk Away

Companies that find themselves in this category are not ready for investment at the current time.

This happens quite often.

Many businesses think that what they lack is capital. But often, inadequate capital is only part of the problem.

However, this may be no fault of the business owner.

When a business is in the bootstrap mode for an extended period, there may not have been a lot of resources to dedicate to efficiency and process optimization.

This could mean that administrative filings have fallen through the cracks, or that there are more manual processes that are more subject to human area.

Scenario 1

The Shiny Parts:

- The owners are working hard on the business.

- The business is generating revenue (even if uneven).

The Warts:

- The business has some state or local registration or certification issues.

- The business has a poor understanding of how they make money.

- The business has a poor understanding of how much money they are making.

- The business is understaffed, or the owner is the only worker.

- There is a significant amount of operational inefficiency.

- Revenue is very unpredictable or sporadic.

Scenario 2

The Shiny Parts:

- The business is already in existence.

The Warts:

- The business has some state or local registration or certification issues.

- The business is not generating revenue.

- The business is winging it—or they have little to no operational protocol.

- The business is open, yet there is very little name recognition or consumer base.

The investments in this category have the potential to be good businesses; however; it is still too soon to tell.

They have some basic business operations issues to work out before pulling in an investor.

There may be an opportunity to come on board as a co-founder or co-owner, but that will likely require a more significant investment of both time and money.

Do not fall for the allure of putting in a small amount of capital in exchange for a large percentage of the business. You are likely to own a large portion of something that yields a negative return and delivers significant headaches.

Know When To Run Away

The Shiny Parts:

- There are no apparent bright spots after further investigation.

The Warts:

- The business is not registered or has been ordered to close due to violations.

- Initial information provided does not match the documentation that was provided.

- The business or the owner does not have a good reputation in the community they are looking to serve.

- The business or the owner has outstanding judgments, litigation or IRS debt.

While this might seem like a no-brainer, many investors fall for the diamond in the rough or the savior narrative.

The diamond in the rough and savior narratives will make you ignore actual red flags, and try to resurrect the business or the owner.

Reviving even a small business is a tough feat.

Remember, you are not a charity, and you aren't resurrecting companies from the dead. You are an investor, and there needs to be a clear path to your making money.

Chapter Summary/Key Takeaways

In this chapter, rather than providing a how-to on reviewing financial statements, we move through real-world scenarios.

In businesses that are ready for investment, the good will significantly outweigh the bad. if this not the case, then take it as an indicator that the business is not completely ready for investment.

CHAPTER SEVEN: SETTING EXPECTATIONS

S etting expectations throughout the entire process is critical to keeping all parties on the same page. It will reduce headaches and save you from miscommunication.

Money Due Date

The first expectation that should be set is when the business will need the investment.

The reply from the business will be very telling.

If the business needs the funding with 30 days, this is a red flag and this may not the business that you invest in.

However, some investors may want to meet an urgent/emergent need. If this is the case, you should only make that kind of emergency leap with someone that you have an established relationship with.

One reason is that the timeframe does not leave you with much time to verify information independently, and that is a problem.

In these cases, the funding is less likely to be fueling growth and is more of a bailout.

In rare cases, it is for gap funding for an event or promotion, but you still need to take time to investigate. So, what should be your investment timeline?

I suggest 45-90 days, depending on the complexity of the investment.

This time frame should allow you time to conduct all of the interviews, visits, and data verification necessary. It also gives you time to move funds if needed.

Keep in mind that if you can complete your process sooner, and you are satisfied that you are well informed about the business and all its intricacies, then you are free to make the investment.

Easy Does It

DO NOT FEEL PRESSURED!

Businesses can make you feel like you have to move now. You both need each other, but high-pressure tactics are not a good sign.

It could be revealing that the money is more desperately needed than originally presented.

A common approach is the FOMO or fear of missing out talk line. This can look like "act now because I only allow a few people in" or, we have a line of investors throwing money at us.

If things are moving too fast, just pass on the opportunity.

What You Really Want

Be upfront with what you want in return, and why you want to invest.

Do not feel the need to over-explain yourself, or create some grandiose long-term vision.

It is completely acceptable to say- I saw this as a good investment opportunity, and I think I can make a return on my money.

If you are in this to make money, be comfortable with that.

It can be difficult in some communities to be upfront and vocal about your desire to prosper financially, but this does not make you a predator, and you should turn a deaf ear to anyone who speaks of your efforts in this way.

If you want to be an active part of the business, then it is vital to be clear about what that means.

Does that mean you will be coming by every day?

Does it mean you want to have a look at the books on a set interval?

Does it mean you want to help with the strategy and execution behind the scenes?

Conversely, do you wish to remain unbothered and simply receive the agreed-upon payments?

Communicating this directly is important.

Length Of Time

The next expectation that needs to be set is how long you want to be an investor.

This will be dependent on your risk tolerance, industry, and personality.

If you are just looking to get your feet wet, then a shorter term may be more suitable.

If you are investing in a start-up, this is likely going to be a longer timeframe likely to be higher than three years.

When deciding how long you want to stay in, consider whether you are expecting a large return or something more marginal.

If you are looking to double your money in a year, that is not a realistic expectation.

Longer investment horizons offer a more significant opportunity for more substantial returns. This does not mean that if you invest longer, then you will always make more.

Furthermore, it would be best if you gave whatever improvements that were made to the business time to work.

Unless you are offering working capital for a product or inventory that already has purchase orders, you will have to invest for longer than six months.

I suggest a 12-15-month initial term for main street investments and 2-4 years for venture investments.

This will give you time to look at the trend, and an option to pull all of your money out without a penalty.

While these expectations may be slightly tweaked depending on the particular circumstances, be firm in what you expect.

There are very few right or wrong answers when it comes to your expectations, be sure to stick to your guns, and find the opportunity that best suits you.

Return

The final expectation to set prior and evaluate is the amount of return that you want.

The average check written by individual angel investors is a little more than $36,000, and the median is $25,000. However, there is a broad range of check sizes, from $5,000 to $100,000 (Hudson, 2017).

The report also shows differences in investment sizes by region, length of time investing, by background, and by gender.

Since 1923, the average return in the stock market (S&P 500) has been 12% (Reuters, 2013).

Angel investors experience higher returns, but they are not quick turnarounds.

Angel investing can be risky business. Most prior studies posit that 5-10 percent of investments will be economically profitable. In the American Angel, investors said on average, 11 percent of their total portfolio yielded a positive exit.

A study conducted in 2014 about angel investors by the Ewing Marion Kauffman Foundation, and the Angel Capital Education Foundation, found that angel investor exits generated 2.6 times the invested capital in 3.5 years from investment to exit.

This study highlights two key observations:

1- The rate of return can be higher on angel investments.

2- 2- These investments are longer-term investments.

Based on this let's do some quick math—

A $10,000 investment would yield $26,000 over 3.5 years or just over $7,400 per year ($619/mo.)—Not a bad return.

All evidence suggests that angel investors can expect approximately 2.5X return over time.

So, when thinking about how much return to expect, 2.5X is an excellent place to start.

Keep in mind that if you want to pull out of an investment earlier than the 2-3-year mark, you will need to consider a lower multiple.

The 2.5X return should act as a guide when looking at the projections.

In the next section, we will discuss the deal structure as the structure of the deal will have a direct impact on your returns.

Chapter Summary/Key Takeaways

In this chapter, we discuss setting your expectations. Upfront and decisive is the name of the game.

If there is too much ambiguity, then you will likely not have an optimal experience.

If you find it challenging to decide exactly where you stand, give yourself time. You are in no rush to invest.

When in doubt, circle back to your financial audit and examine what your return goals might be, and that might point you in the right direction.

PART III: THE DEAL

"You must never try to make all the money that's in a deal. Let the other fellow make some money too, because if you have a reputation for always making all the money, you won't have many deals."

– J. Paul Getty

CHAPTER EIGHT:
LET'S MAKE A DEAL

One of the fundamental principles of investing is low risk = low reward, and high risk = high reward.

Identifying risk can be tough. Even more challenging is how to determine what the probability that an owner or founder will be successful is.

This is where investing in what you know is particularly helpful because as much as we can apply logic or math to investment, the more you know, the quicker your gut instincts will kick in, and help guide you through decision making.

In chapter six, we moved through several scenarios. These scenarios were ranked from the best case to the worst-case scenarios.

The risk would correlate with those scenarios.

The "hold 'em" scenarios correspond to low risk, while the "runaway" scenarios are the highest risk. Therefore, an existing business with steady revenue that is looking to grow has less risk than a startup venture with no income at all.

If you have moved through the diligence process in a careful, thoughtful manner, then you are in complete control of the strength and weaknesses of the business.

In this chapter, we will discuss how to structure your deal to increase your return, and how to reduce your risks.

Debt Versus Equity

When speaking in terms of investment, most people automatically think that what they receive in return is an ownership stake or equity.

Instead of crafting your deal for equity, you may want to consider setting it up like a debt, in other words, like a loan.

All states have established guidelines for loans, including providing ways to secure it.

Most people are familiar with collateral and how that can be used in a loan.

In many cases, you file a document called a Universal Code 1 (UCC-1). By filling this document, you as an investor moves from a general creditor to a secured creditor.

This filing says that you (the investor) has an interest in the specified property.

This structure could be especially valuable for main street investments.

Similarly, rather than just taking equity in an early-stage company, a convertible note allows for repayment, and warrants allow you an option to buy common stock for next to nothing in the future should they be worth something.

In an early investment, this could be very valuable because as an angel investor, you are putting some of the first money in. This is in hopes that you help the company move to the next stage and attract a larger check to help them on the way.

In this scenario, exercising your warrant may mean getting an even larger reward for taking the early risk.

Terms

After deciding on whether you wish to make your investment more like a debt, or choose to go with equity, you need to present the terms to the business.

This can be done in several forms: verbally, via a term sheet, or a commitment letter.

In most instances, I don't advise the terms to be presented verbally. Putting terms in writing is critical.

A term sheet is a one-page document that outlines the deal. This document should spell out the high level (and important) details.

A commitment letter has significantly more details.

I recommend a term sheet for the simple deals, small investments and main street investments, and the commitment letter for startup investments that will be for a longer period, especially those opportunities that you believe will be high growth (high return) investments.

A term sheet should have the following details:

- **The business**: In this section, you should be detailing the business and the proprietary products of value.

Define this very carefully as you do not wish to have the business make significant changes before the investment is made.

- **Consideration**: This is where you identify what you are giving (money/expertise/network), and what you are getting (equity, monthly payments, board seat).

This section can also include additional requirements like allowing control of customer lists or securing the supply chain.

- **Purchase Price**: This could be the price that you are acquiring shares for, or the amount that will be invested in the business.

- **Payment Terms**: Simply put, how do you plan to get your money back?

This is where you define any interests, due payment dates, payment intervals, when the payments should begin, and when they should end.

This section should be as detailed as possible.

- **Due Diligence**: Yes, you have already conducted diligence, but after presenting a term sheet, you may want to forward certain documents or agreements to a financial advisor and maybe your attorney for review.

The diligence period after a term sheet is presented a bit more defined. In real estate, this could be anywhere from 30-180 days, depending on the complexity of the work that needs to be completed.

In most cases, this second phase of diligence is less than 45 days.

Be sure to check with all the people who will be conducting reviews on your behalf to be sure that they can complete the work within the set time frame.

A savvy business owner may require that you pay a penalty if you back out as compensation for the loss of time or the effort put in.

A key provision in this section is that the information has to be acceptable to the expert.

This means while you may have done an initial review, a professional may offer a different opinion which could mean that you can back out based on those findings.

- **Closing Conditions**: These terms include provisions

like:

-The information will remain valid on the closing date.

-That the owner is properly following all laws and provisions.

-That you, the investor, has procured or has made arrangements for funds to be available to close the deal.

-The owner has the authority to complete the transaction.

-The investor is satisfied with the due diligence findings.

- **Governing Law**: This defines the court where any disputes will be resolved.

In most cases, as the investor, you should choose the state that is most convenient for you. In some exceptional cases, you may be choosing a state that has the most business-friendly laws.

Your attorney can give you the best guidance on where you should select.

If necessary, you may need to state that business will be conducted in the English language.

- **Fees and Expenses**: If there are costs associated with completing the deal, then it is recommended that each side covers its expenses.

For business owners, this keeps costs down, and for investors, this helps in being decisive.

Paralysis by analysis can be a real thing, so capping your expenditures is wise.

- **Binding or Non-binding Terms**: Term sheets can

come in two varieties: binding and non-binding.

A binding term sheet means that each part is held to this agreement.

Furthermore, barring a limited set of circumstances, the deal will go through.

A binding term sheet holds more weight than a non-binding version. However, there are reasons why a non-binding term sheet should be presented.

If there is significant diligence left to do, or if the deal is contingent on other factors or conditions being met, a non-binding term sheet can give both sides more opportunity to walk away.

If the term sheet is binding, the term sheet should prohibit the business from conducting any other ownership stakes or making other transactions that might change the return profile.

- **Confidentiality**: Yes, this is in addition to the NDA (Non-Disclosure Agreement) that you signed previously.

This section requires that each side agrees that this term sheet is for a potential transaction between the investor and the owner, and is confidential.

This includes both the specific terms, including investment amount, and return or interest.

In some cases, it may be wise to keep confidential that the deal is being negotiated or considered.

- **Expiration Date**: Any terms offered should expire.

This helps not to waste either side's time. Most term sheets are only valid for 14-30 days after the stated diligence period is over.

Term sheets are negotiable. Be sure to give the business time to review the terms.

The terms that are set in the term sheet should have an expiration date. That date should give the business enough time to consider the terms properly.

While there is no need to rush, 14 days is generally enough time for review.

The business may want to amend some of the terms. Any amendments have to make sense and be aligned with the goals and expectations that were set.

Two popular terms that the business may fight to have amended are the amount of capital to be invested and the ownership stake.

While these are popular negotiation points, they are linked together. The relationship between the investment amount and the ownership stake is determined in most terms by the business valuation.

However, valuations can be very tricky.

For startups that do not have previous capital invested or revenue generation, valuations may not hold much value.

Many startups will come with their own valuation numbers. If you are the first money in, it is a better idea to invest your funds via a convertible note. This will allow you to convert to an ownership stake at a later date when a proper valuation can be reached.

For main street businesses, a valuation can be reached using several methods.

An effortless way to find the value of a business is through business insurance. Depending on the type of policy, a valuation for the business may have been reached for insurance purposes. This may overvalue the business, but it could be a starting point.

Understanding Business Valuations

Method 1: Asset-based

The asset-based method evaluates the business's assets and liabilities.

To calculate the value of the business, you have to find the difference between assets and liabilities.

When you use the asset-based method, you look at your business as being made up of smaller parts. Some parts add value to your company. Other parts add debts to your business.

Items that add value are assets, while liabilities are the debts your company owes to creditors.

There are some pros and cons to this method.

This method is popular for asset-heavy businesses-those businesses that own property or pieces of equipment.

If the business owns the property outright, and there are no other outstanding lenders or liens, this methodology could be beneficial.

If the equipment is being leased, this method is not very useful as the value of the asset will be off-set by the debt it carries.

Also, many main street businesses may find themselves in an asset poor situation.

The asset method is similar to how a bank would decide if a business is eligible for a loan. The assets would be likely termed the collateral.

If you use this method to value the business, you may want to consider tying your investment to those assets for security.

To determine the value of the business, subtract liabilities from the assets.

Here's a general example, if the business has $100,000 in assets and $30,000 in liabilities, the value of the business is $70,000 ($100,000 – $30,000 = $70,000).

A con to this method is determining the value of the assets (the liabilities are easy, bills and payments help you determine this quickly). The challenge with finding the value of equipment or property often lies with finding the book value.

However, the asset-based method could be beneficial if the business needs to be sold quickly, or if you are looking to invest enough in the business to control a significant stake.

If the owner of a business is relying heavily on this method, the business may not be very healthy. This method generally keeps the value low which could be good for the investor but keep in mind that there may be some significant warts that warrant a fast sell and not much price haggling.

Method 2: Market

The method will be familiar if you have ever purchased a home.

The "comparables" of houses in the area are often pulled to help verify, and validate the value of the home to be purchased.

The market method compares your business to similar companies that have already been sold.

Here is a simple example:

Let's say the business you are looking to invest in is a salon, and other salons in the area are selling for an average of $60,000. Using the market method, the business is worth about $60,000.

The market method offers an amount close to the fair market value.

Finding "true" comparable businesses may be challenging. A proper comparable business should be of similar size, revenue generation, and possibly even geographical location. The more factors that match, the more relevant the valuation will be.

This type of data in a general public search is hard to come by. Most of the data that can be easily found will be of public companies which from a size and scope perspective are not relevant even if the industry is the same; a McDonald's is not the same as a local family burger spot.

There is a general business principle that a target is only worth what someone is willing to pay for it. This can cut both ways for an investor. If there is another investor or offer on the table, and the other investor is willing to pay more, then by default, the business is worth more- the competition drives up the price.

If you are the only investor, then what you are willing to pay sets the price.

While this can be exciting, be fair and reasonable as you are looking to be an angel investor, not a vulture.

The value of the business depends on the market. This can pose an issue if the market the business is in is shrinking, or the economy is down.

If this is the case, this can depress the value; this may be a good thing for an investor as the dollars invested will buy more of the business.

Method 3: Income

The income method is what I recommend. The income method looks at the business's financial history and financial health.

Using all of the financial documents that you requested and gathered during due diligence, you can evaluate the business's financial health.

With the income method, you look at the businesses past profit, revenue, and cash flow using your profit and loss statement, or previous tax returns.

Use at least three years if available, and pay close attention to the trend.

Notice if the revenue line is going up every year, staying the same, decreasing, or all over the place.

Then take a look at the profit (the line that says *"after all expenses were taken out"*). Look at the same trends. Evaluate if the two lines show the same trends.

If the revenue is going up, and the profit is going down, that could be a sign that the increase in sales costs more to achieve.

If the revenue is going down or staying steady and the profit trend is going up, then this could be a sign that the business is becoming more efficient.

By examining the previous years and looking at the trends, especially the percent growth year over year, then you can project what the revenue and profits may be for the next few years during your investment.

If the company has only been in business for a year or less, then you can use the month over month revenue and profits. However, use the month over month number to project months, not several years as it could be misleading.

With this method, the value of the business is the amount of money the business makes.

When making an offer for the business, your price will likely be the average revenue or profit number per year, multiplied by the number of years the owner is charging.

Quick Math

If the average revenue per year equals $250,000, an offer of $1.25M would be paying for the "revenue lost" to the owner for 5 years.

A Quick Note on Revenue, Earnings, Receipts, Profit

As previously discussed, top-line revenue in a company's financial statements is the money received before a product or service.

It is also called receipts.

Bottom line revenue, on the other hand, is the number that is left after all the costs of running the company, and making the product, including taxes are deducted. This is also known as profit.

There is another common line used for valuation, and that is the EBIT and EBITDA line.

EBIT is earnings before interest and taxes, while EBITDA is Earnings before interest, taxes, depreciation, and amortization.

Sometimes, the earnings are adjusted to take out income taxes, non-recurring income and expenses, non-operating income and expenses, depreciation and amortization, interest expense or interest income, or owner compensation.

Method 4: Valuing a Business with Multiples of Earnings

In most cases, EBIT (earnings before interest and taxes) is the measure used for the earnings number.

Similar to the previous approach, multiple is used to determine the value.

The "multiple" is the number you multiply the baseline number by.

The market or an industry peer determines the multiple. There are some national standards, depending on industry type and business size.

The multiple can be positive or negative. A negative multiple would be appropriate if there are significant negative factors present. This would result in the valuation of the company being less than one.

Let's say the multiple is two. If the earnings of the business are $900,000, the multiples of earnings calculation mean the business may be valued for sale at $1,800,000.

Keep in mind that according to Bizbuysell, the average business sells for around 0.6 times its annual revenue, nationally.

Think of the average or profit revenue line as the baseline or 1.

Note: As an investor, you will want to use the profit line as the baseline. The business owner will want to use the revenue line.

As you are moving through due diligence, you should be noting the overall pros and cons. These are very valuable when the time comes for determining the valuation.

Another way to look at it is that you are "discounting" the money they have made. Generally, this would not be a business that you make your very first investment in as this type of business would be a salvage operation that has potential but will require work.

An interesting note on valuations is that very rarely do both the business and the investor 100% agree on it.

This is understandable as both sides are motivated by different factors. In addition to emotional attachment and sweat equity, a business owner wants and needs the value of the business to be higher.

This will mean a higher sale price if they are looking to liquidate the business, or a small amount of ownership that they are giving to an investor.

The investor wants the value at the time of investment to be lower because it presents the opportunity to own more for less.

Let's walk through a specific situation. If you as an investor offered to invest $10,000 in exchange for a 10% stake in a business, this by default means that you are valuing the business at $100,000. *$10,000 multiplied by 10 (to make 100%) equals $100,000.*

If you offered the same business $10,000 for a 50% stake, then you are valuing the business at $20,000.

Once the terms have been jointly agreed to, both parties should sign the term sheet.

Chapter Summary/Key Takeaways

In this chapter, we discuss the terms. At this phase, it is all about the details.

This is where you are proposing a business marriage. There should be no gaps in the verbal conversations and what is now down on paper.

Each of the sections is vital, and they should not be skipped for the sake of making the term sheet shorter.

Be brief but don't sell yourself short. Put it all in writing.

CHAPTER NINE: PAPERWORK

After the term sheet is signed, there is a brief wait before the deal is finalized.

In this time, use all your powers of observation. Make sure that you are keeping tabs on the businesses, making sure that there are no significant changes to business, including the staff or personnel, the building, the signage, marketing etc.

Look out for large expenditures or purchases. Also, observe the owner's behavior.

Do not feel pressured to sign an agreement sooner than what is allotted for the second level of diligence in the term sheet.

During the waiting period, your attorney should be drafting your agreement.

Be sure to let the attorney know how much time he has to get a draft out. This is especially important if the attorney did not draft the term sheet.

If you are looking to keep the cost of the drafting low, then be sure not to require a rush drafting job, and provide all the information that the attorney will need to give you a quality document.

Remember a comprehensive the term sheet is 50% of what makes up a solid agreement.

While I do not recommend that you draft your own agreement, you should know what a comprehensive agreement looks like, and what sections should be included.

The Description of Parties appears at the beginning of the document. This section provides the following information about the buyer(s) and the seller(s):

- Legal names

- Addresses

- Phone numbers

Description Of Business

Also known as the Sellers' Representations and Warranties, this section provides a detailed description of the following things:

- Location(s) of the business

- Purpose of the business

- Services the business provides

- Products the company sells

- Business entity under which the company operates

- Management structure of the business

- Management systems the business uses

- Past, present, and future financials

- Types of customers who come into the business or who use the business's services

Description Of Sale

Absolutely vital to the purchase agreement, this section identifies the following:

- Type of sale (Asset, Stock, Earnout, Seller-Carried Note, and/or Seller Employment)

- Description of every asset, stock, and item included in the sale

- Description of every asset, stock, and item excluded from the sale

Transfer Of Property

Hinging upon the description of sellable assets, stocks, and items, this section can include the following:

- Seller's Agreement to Sell the listed assets, stocks, and items

- Buyer's Agreement to Purchase the listed assets, stocks, and items

Purchase Price

Once the document identifies what is, and what is not included in the business sale, the purchase agreement will outline the following:

- Price buyers are paying for the listed assets, items, and/or stocks

- How the buyer plans to pay for the business (can include outside financing, seller-carried notes, seller employment, and/or stock buyouts)

Assumption Of Risk And Liabilities (Sometimes

One-And-The-Same As Covenants)

This section often dictates which party assumes responsibility for the following risks and liabilities before and after closing:

- Product loss
- Loss of revenue
- Tax liabilities
- Third-party fees
- Loan obligations
- Vendor obligations
- Employee salaries

Covenants (Often Split Into Buyer Agreements And Seller Agreements)

If separated from the Assumption of Risk section, many of the protective clauses I mentioned can appear in this section. Look for any:

- **Indemnification**- In business, indemnification is a contractual obligation in which one party agrees to protect another party for financial loss.
- **Business Conduct**- This clause typically states that the business will be run in compliance with all laws.

It may also outline what behaviors will not be tolerated, or what might happen if legal/ criminal action is taken against one of the owners.

- **Non-Compete**- This section will prohibit the owners from starting, participating, or promoting another business in the same sector.

This section may also attempt to restrict the owner from owning a similar business within a specified period.

- **Non-Solicit**- This section will prohibit from selling to or attempting to steal customers, employees, vendors, or other partners from the business.

- **Confidentiality**- This section will protect the data and information of the business from being shared.

- **Intellectual Property**- Generally, the business will own any patents, trademarks, and/or copyrights, even if the individual owner came up with the idea.

A critical section in this agreement details what the seller/ existing business owners responsibilities are after the agreement is signed.

- Clarify the seller's role within the business after the sale

- Determine who will teach and train the new owners and any new employees

- Specify who will notify vendors and customers that the business has transferred ownership

Participation Or Absence Of Brokers

If buyers and/or sellers have engaged a third-party facilitator or professional during the sale process, the business purchase agreement will detail who those professionals are, and who is responsible for covering their fees. This does include attorney fees.

Conditions

The conditions section will directly mirror the term sheet as all of the conditions should be the same, including what needs to happen for sale to be complete and any due diligence.

Exit

This is important to detail carefully. There should be clarity on how you will exit as an investor even if you plan to be a part of the business indefinitely.

Closing

This section details the when and where the agreement will be executed.

It will provide: a location for the closing, list the time closing will occur, issues title transfers (if applicable), and specify what monies will be paid upon closing.

Miscellaneous

The name of the section is a bit misleading. This section is neither unimportant nor unnecessary. This section can include:

Reveal purchase price allocations.

Adjust the purchase price to reflect prorated business expenses, inventory, or accounts receivable on closing day.

Outline how to resolve party disputes if they occur.

Signatures

Appearing at the end of the document, the buyers and sellers will sign their agreement to the terms and conditions outlined in the document.

A representative attorney, banker, broker, or CEPA in attendance at the closing will also sign as a witness, and notarize the buyer and seller signatures.

Exhibits/Appendices

This section will include other agreements that would have been requested during the initial diligence period. Any of these documents may be included in this section:

- Financial statements and reports
- The Letter of Intent
- Signed agreements
- Leasehold agreements/transfers
- Vendor agreements/transfers
- Asset valuations
- Owner and/or employee biographies
- Industry reports
- Marketing plans and contracts

It is a good idea that you keep all these documents together, so putting them into the agreement can save you some organizational headaches down the line.

Once the first draft is shared with the business owner, be sure to allow them and their attorney to read, review and make edits.

Do not get frustrated if there are a few rounds of edits. It is far better to have everyone in agreement and on the same page than to encounter a costly conflict down the road.

Chapter Summary/Key Takeaways

In this chapter, we discuss what should be included in your full agreement.

When doing this, a good attorney is your best friend. They will cover all the bases and eventualities.

As the saying goes, they will draft in the sunshine, and prepare for the rain.

CHAPTER TEN:
THE EXIT

The exit (hopefully) is the fun part of the process. This is the part where your bet and early investment should pay off. If you have followed the procedure carefully, the exit will not be a surprise to either party.

In a typical main street investment, you should be simply cashing out of the business and ownership will likely be back to the original owner.

In a smooth process, the current value of the business will be determined, and your share will be calculated and, then paid.

Unfortunately, in the real world, other things can happen.

Here are a few scenarios that you may find yourself in.

Death

If the owner of the business dies, the operating agreement will spell out who will assume the business, or if it will continue.

If the new owner wishes to exit, or has no desire to continue the business, you can cash out before they sell.

This could save you the headache of dealing with a new owner.

Alternatively, if you have had a good experience with the business, you may want to take it over. They may require upfront cash but depending on the new owner, you may be able to structure a buy-out of their interest over time.

Bankruptcy Or Business Closure

Stuff happens. Whether the cause is an economic recession, a declining neighborhood, or bad business management, the result is the same.

In this scenario, you are much more likely to take a financial loss.

If the closure is voluntary, meaning not due to a bank foreclosure or another creditor forcing closure, you may be in a position to sell assets and retain some cash.

If the closure is forced, you as an owner will likely have a second- or third-line position for being made whole.

Acquisition

A successful business may attract potential buyers.

The majority owner may receive an offer that they could not turn down.

If in your agreement, the owner cannot sell without your approval or notifying you—you will have a say in the sale.

If you have no rights to refuse the sale or a first right of refusal (the option to buy the business first), you may want to sell your shares prior to acquisition as there will likely be changes to the business.

Personal Reasons

As an investor, life can happen. Certain personal issues may call for you to sell your interest.

The reasons can be a personal financial strain, and you need to find some cash.

A new baby, husband, or relocation can also mean that your investment appetite or risk tolerance has changed.

If this is the case, then you may not be able to capture the full value of what your shares are worth.

Remember that you should always prepare for the exit at the beginning.

When drafting your full agreement, including these scenarios of an untimely exit can save you a lot of time, negotiation, and conflict.

Chapter Summary/Key Takeaways

In this chapter, we talked about the exit. This is the whole point of being an investor.

You are making a financial investment and accepting the risks to make a return.

If you are acting as an investor, you will not be looking to be a part of the business forever.

You are not looking to run a business; you are looking for financial gain.

EPILOGUE/ CONCLUSION

This book is intended to be a guide for first-time investors to get involved in the investment process.

Often, communities of color are underinvested in until another group decides to see the value.

There are many members of the community that can fill the capital void, and help to build value where they live.

I hope after reading this guide, the process has been demystified, and you realize that we do not need anyone to come and save us—there are angels already among us.

APPENDIX

Glossary of Terms

Sample Due Diligence Questions

Example Questions for Investment Group Formation

GLOSSARY OF TERMS

1. **Accounts Payable**

Accounts payable is a business finance 101 term. This represents your small business's obligations to pay debts owed to lenders, suppliers, and creditors.

Sometimes referred to as A/P or AP for short, accounts payable can be short or long term depending upon the type of credit provided to the business by the lender.

2. Accounts Receivable

Also known as A/R (or AR, good guess), accounts receivables is another business finance 101 term. It refers to the money owed to your small business by others for goods or services rendered.

These accounts are labeled as assets because they represent a legal obligation for the customer to pay you cash for their short-term debt.

3. Accrual Basis

The accrual basis of accounting is an accounting method of recording income when it's actually earned, and expenses when they actually occur.

Accrual basis of accounting is the most common approach used by larger businesses to record, and maintain financial transactions.

4. Accruals

A business finance term and definition referring to expenses that have been incurred but haven't yet been recorded in the business books. Wages and payroll taxes are common examples.

5. Asset

This business finance key term is anything that has value—whether tangible or intangible—and is owned by the business is considered an asset.

Typical items listed as business assets are cash on hand, accounts receivable, buildings, equipment, inventory, and anything else that can be turned into cash.

6. Balance Sheet

Along with three other reports relating to the financial health of your small business, the balance sheet is essential information that gives a "snapshot" of the company's net worth at any given time.

The report is a summary of the business assets and liabilities.

7. Bookkeeping

A method of accounting that involves the timely recording of all financial transactions for the business.

8. Capital

This refers to the overall wealth of a business, as demonstrated by its cash accounts, assets, and investments.

Often called "fixed capital," it refers to the long-term worth of the business.

Capital can be tangible, like durable goods, buildings, and equipment, or intangible such as intellectual property.

9. Working Capital

Not to be confused with fixed capital, working capital is another business finance 101 term.

It consists of the financial resources necessary for maintaining the day-to-day operation of the business. Working capital, by definition, is the business's cash on hand, or instruments that you can convert to cash quickly.

10. Cash Flow

Every business needs cash to operate. The business finance term and definition 'cash flow' refers to the amount of operating cash that "flows" through the business, and affects the business's liquidity.

Cash flow reports reflect activity for a specified period, usually one accounting period or one month.

Maintaining tight control of cash flow is especially important if your small business is new since ready cash can be limited until the business begins to grow and produce more working capital.

11. Cash Flow Projections

Future business decisions will depend on your educated cash flow projections.

To plan for upcoming expenditures and working capital, you need to depend on previous cash flow patterns.

These patterns will give you a comprehensive look at how, and when you receive and spend your cash.

This information is the key to unlock informed, accurate cash flow projections.

12. Depreciation

The value of any asset can be said to depreciate when it loses some of that value in increments over time.

Depreciation occurs due to wear and tear.

Various methods of depreciation are used by businesses to decrease the recorded value of assets.

13. Fixed Asset

A tangible, long-term asset used for the business, and not expected to be sold or otherwise converted into cash during the current or upcoming fiscal year is called a fixed asset.

Fixed assets are items like furniture, computer equipment, equipment, and real estate.

14. Gross Profit

This business finance term and definition can be calculated as total sales (income), less the costs (expenses) directly related to those sales.

Raw materials, manufacturing expenses, labor costs, marketing, and transportation of goods are all included in expenses.

15. Income Statement

Here is one of the four most essential reports lenders and investors want to see when evaluating the viability of your small business.

It is also called a profit and loss statement, and it addresses the business's bottom line, reporting how much the business has earned and spent over a given period.

The result will be either a net gain or a net loss.

16. Intangible Asset

A business asset that is non-physical is considered intangible.

These assets can be items like patents, goodwill, and intellectual property.

17. Liability

This business finance key term is a legal obligation to repay or otherwise settle a debt. Liabilities are considered either current (payable within one year or less) or long-term (payable after one year) and are listed on a business's balance sheet.

A business's accounts payable, wages, taxes, and accrued expenses are all considered liabilities.

18. Liquidity

Liquidity is an indicator of how quickly an asset can be turned into cash for full market value. The more liquid your assets, the more financial flexibility you have.

19. Profit & Loss Statement

See "Income Statement" above.

20. Statement Of Cash Flow

One of the essential documents required by lenders and investors that shows a summary of the actual collection of revenue, and payment of expenses for your business.

The statement of cash flow should reflect activity in the areas of operating, investing, and financing, and should be an integral part of your financial statement package.

21. Statement Of Shareholders' Equity

If you have chosen to fund your small business with equity financing, and you have established shares and shareholders as part of the controlling interests, you are obligated to provide a financial report that shows changes in the equity section of your balance sheet.

22. Annual Percentage Rate

The business finance term and definition APR represents the real yearly cost of a loan, including all interest and fees.

The total amount of interest to be paid is based on the original amount loaned, or the principal, and is represented in percentage form.

When shopping for the right loan for your small business, you should know the APR for the loan in question. This figure can be very helpful in comparing one financial tool with another since it represents the actual cost of borrowing.

23. Appraisal

Just like your real estate appraisal when buying a house, an appraisal is a professional opinion of market value.

When closing a loan for your small business, you will probably need one or more of the three types of appraisals: real estate, equipment, and business value.

24. Balloon Loan

A loan that is structured in a way that the small business owner makes regular repayments on a predetermined schedule, and one much larger payment or balloon payment, at the end.

These can be attractive to new businesses because the payments are smaller at the outset when the business is more likely to be facing strict financial constraints.

However, be sure that your business will be capable of making that last balloon payment since it will be a large one.

25. Bankruptcy

This federal law is used as a tool for businesses or individuals who are having severe financial challenges.

It provides a plan for reduction and repayment of debts over time, or an opportunity to eliminate the majority of the outstanding debts completely.

Turning to bankruptcy should be given careful thought because it will hurt the business credit score.

26. Bootstrapping

Using your own money to finance the start-up and growth of your small business. Think of it as being your own investor.

Once the business is up and running successfully, the business finance term and definition bootstrapping refers to the use of profits earned to reinvest in the business.

27. Business Credit Report

Just like you have a personal credit report that lenders look at to determine risk factors for making personal loans, businesses also generate credit reports.

These are maintained by credit bureaus that record information about a business's financial history.

Items like how large the company is, how long it has been in business, amount and type of credit issued to the business, how credit has been managed, and any legal filings (i.e., bankruptcy) are all questions addressed by the business credit report.

Lenders, investors, and insurance companies use these reports to evaluate risk exposure and financial health of a business.

28. Business Credit Score

A business credit score is calculated based on the information found in the business credit report.

Using a specialized algorithm, business credit scoring companies take into account all the information found on your credit report, and give your small business a credit score.

Also called a commercial credit score, this number is used by various lenders and suppliers to evaluate your creditworthiness.

29. Collateral

Any asset that you pledge as security for a loan instrument is called collateral.

Lenders often require collateral as a way to make sure they won't lose money if your business defaults on the loan.

When you pledge an asset for collateral, it becomes subject to seizure by the lender if you fail to meet the requirements of the loan documents.

30. Credit Limit

When a lender offers a business line of credit, it usually comes with a credit limit, or a maximum amount that you can use at any given time.

It is said that you reach your credit limit or "max out" your credit when you borrow up to or exceed that number.

A business line of credit can be especially useful if your business is seasonal, or if the income is extremely unpredictable.

It is one of the fastest ways to access cash for emergencies.

31. Debt Consolidation

If your small business has several loans with various payments, you might want to consider a business debt consolidation loan.

It is a process that lets you combine multiple loans into a single loan.

The advantages are possibly reducing the interest rates on the borrowed funds, as well as lowering the total amount you repay each month.

Businesses use this tool to help improve cash flow.

32. Debt Service Coverage Ratio

The business finance term and definition debt service coverage ratio (DSCR) is the ratio of cash your small business has available for paying or servicing its debt.

Debt payments include making principal and interest payments on the loan you are requesting.

Generally speaking, if your DSCR is above 1, your business has enough income to meet its debt requirements.

33. Debt Financing

When you borrow money from a lender and agree to repay the principal with interest in regular payments for a specified period, you're using debt financing.

Traditionally, it has been the most common form of funding for small businesses.

Debt financing can include borrowing from banks, business credit cards, lines of credit, personal loans, merchant cash advances, and invoice financing.

This method creates a debt that must be repaid, but lets you maintain sole control of your business.

34. Equity Financing

The act of using investor funds in exchange for a piece or "share" of your business is another way to raise capital.

These funds can come from friends, family, angel investors, or venture capitalists.

Before deciding to use equity financing to raise the cash necessary for your business, determine how much control you are willing to share when it comes to decision-making and philosophy.

Some investors will also want voting rights.

35. Fico Score

A FICO score is another type of credit score used by potential lenders for evaluating the wisdom of entering a contract with you and your business. The Fair Isaac Corporation created it, hence the name FICO.

FICO scores comprise a substantial part of the credit report that lenders use to assess credit risk.

36. Financial Statements

An integral part of the loan application process is furnishing information that shows your business is a good credit risk.

The standard financial statement packet includes four main reports: the income statement, the balance sheet, the statement of cash flow, and the statement of shareholders' equity, if you have shareholders.

Lenders and investors want to see that your business is well-balanced with assets and liabilities, has positive cash flow, and will have the capital to make expected repayments.

37. Fixed Interest Rate

The interest rate on a loan that is established in the beginning and does not change for the lifetime of the loan is said to be fixed.

Loans with fixed interest rates are appealing to small business owners because the repayment amounts are consistent and easier to budget for in the future.

38. Floating Interest Rate

In contrast to the business finance term and definition fixed rate, the floating interest rate will change with market fluctuations.

Also referred to as variable rates or adjustable rates, these amounts may often start out lower than the fixed-rate percentages. This makes them more appealing in the short term if the market is trending down.

39. Guarantor

When starting a new small business, lenders might want you to provide a guarantor. This is an individual who guarantees to cover the balance owed on a debt if you or your business cannot meet the repayment obligation.

40. Interest Rate

All loans and other lending instruments are assigned the business finance key term interest rates. This is a percentage of the principal amount charged by the lender for the use of its money.

Interest rates represent the current cost of borrowing.

41. Invoice Factoring Or Financing

If your business has a significant amount of open invoices outstanding, you may contact a factoring company and have them purchase the invoices at a discount.

By raising capital this way, there is no debt, and the factoring company assumes the financial responsibility for collecting the invoice debts.

42. Lien

This business finance term and definition is a creditor's legal claim to the collateral pledged as security for a loan is called a lien.

43. Line Of Credit

A lender may offer you an unsecured amount of funds available for your business to draw on when capital is needed.

This line of credit is considered a short-term funding option, with a maximum amount available.

This pre-approved pool of money is appealing because it gives you quick access to the cash.

44. Loan-To-Value

The LTV comparison is a ratio of the fair market value of an asset compared to the amount of the loan that will fund it.

This is another critical number for lenders who need to know if the value of the asset will cover the loan repayment if your business defaults and fails to pay.

45. Long-Term Debt

Any loan product with a total repayment schedule lasting longer than one year is considered long-term debt.

46. Merchant Cash Advance

A merchant may offer a funding method through a loan based on the business's monthly sales volume. Repayment is made with a percentage of the daily or weekly sales.

These tend to be short-term loans, and are one of the costliest ways to fund your small business.

47. Microloan

Microloans are loans made through nonprofit, community-based organizations, and they are most often for amounts under $50,000.

48. Personal Guarantee

If you're seeking financing for a very new business, and don't have a high-value asset to offer as collateral, you may be asked by the lender to sign a statement of personal guarantee.

In effect, this statement affirms that you, as an individual, will act as guarantor for the business's debt, making you personally liable for the balance of the loan, even if the business fails.

49. Principal

Any loan instrument is made of three parts—the principal, the interest, and the fees.

The principal is a business finance key term and is the original amount that is borrowed or the outstanding balance to be repaid less interest.

It is used to calculate the total interest and fees charged.

50. Revolving Line Of Credit

This business finance term and definition is a funding option and is similar to a standard line of credit.

However, the agreement is to lend a specific amount of money, and once that sum is repaid, it can be borrowed again.

51. Secured Loan

Many lenders will require some form of security when loaning money. When this happens, this business finance term and definition is a secured loan.

The asset being used as collateral for the loan is said to be "securing" the loan.

If your small business defaults on the loan, the lender can then claim the collateral, and use its fair-market value to offset the unpaid balance.

52. Term Loan

These are debt financing tools used to raise needed funds for your small business.

Term loans provide the business with a lump sum of cash upfront in exchange for a promise to repay the principal and interest at specified intervals over a set period.

These are typically longer-term, one-time loans for start-up expenses or costs for established business expansion.

53. Unsecured Loans

Loans that are not backed by collateral are called unsecured loans.

These types of loans represent a higher risk for the lender, so you can expect to pay higher interest rates and have shorter repayment time frames.

Credit cards are an excellent example of unsecured loans that are a good option for small business funding when combined with other financing options.

54. Articles Of Incorporation

This is legal documentation of the business's creation, including name, type of business, and type of business structure or incorporation.

This paperwork is one of the first tasks you will complete when you officially start your business.

Once submitted, your articles of incorporation are kept on file with the appropriate governmental agencies.

55. Business Plan

Your tool for demonstrating how you want to establish your small business, and how you plan to grow it into good financial health.
When writing a business plan, it should include financial, operational, and marketing goals as well as how you plan to get there.

The more specific you are with your business plan, the better prepared you will be in the long run.

56. Employer Identification Number (Ein) Certificate

In order to be more easily identified by the Internal Revenue Service, every business entity is assigned a unique number called an EIN.

When you start your small business, an EIN will be assigned and mailed to the business address.

This number never changes, and you will be asked to furnish it for many reasons.

57. Franchise Agreement

For a small business entrepreneur, entering into a franchise agreement with a larger company can be a way to enter the market-place.

The agreement made between you and the larger company gives you the right to operate as a satellite of the larger company in a defined territory for a given period.

This lets you, the business owner, take advantage of a brand name that's already familiar in the marketplace, and a process or operation that has already been tested

58. Net Worth

This business finance term and definition is an expression of your business's total value, as determined by your total current assets less the total liabilities currently owned by the business.

With your business's most recent balance sheet in hand, you can calculate the net worth using a simple formula: Assets – Liabilities = Net Worth

59. Retained Earnings

Just like it sounds, this term represents any profits earned that are retained in the business.

This can also be referred to as bootstrapping.

60. Tax Lien

If your business fails to pay taxes owed to the designated government entity, namely the IRS, you may find your assets seized by the claim of a tax lien.

The government can not only seize your assets for liquidation to resolve the tax debt, but they can also charge you penalties on the amount you owe.

SAMPLE DUE DILIGENCE QUESTIONS

Sample Due Diligence Questions

*Note not all these questions will be appropriate for every situation

Articles of Incorporation
Bylaws and operating agreements
Shareholder agreements
Minutes of Board of Directors and Shareholder meetings
All documents furnished to shareholders and directors
Certificates from all states and jurisdictions where the company does business

Previous Securities Issuance:

Copies of stock certificates, warrants and option agreements
Complete Stockholder contact information
Number of outstanding shares, dates of issuance, and

percent ownership
All outstanding preferred stock, including covenants
All outstanding options, warrants or convertible securities
Employee stock benefit programs; stock options, stock purchases or others

Audited financial statements since inception
Income statements, balance sheets, cash flow statements
Records of all changes in equity position
Accounting methods and practices
Company prepared monthly or quarterly statements
A three year budget and financial projections
A complete and current business plan
Accounts receivable aging and accounts payable aging
Product or service pricing plans and policies
Revenue and gross margins by product or service
Extraordinary income or expense details
Explanation of any material write-downs or write-offs
A summary of all bad debt experiences
Details of any outstanding contingent liabilities
Accountant report on the company's financial condition

Federal and state income tax returns for the last three years Detail of any tax audits

List of Bank and non-Bank lenders
Joint venture and partnership agreements
License agreements
Purchase agreements
Liens, equipment leases, mortgages or any other outstanding loans
Insurance contracts and agreements
Contracts with suppliers, vendors and customers

Any additional agreements or contracts relevant to the business of the company

Copies of all permits and licenses
Copies of reports made to government agencies
Detail of any inquiries made by any local, state or federal agencies

Description of any current litigation including potential damages
Description of any potential litigation including potential damages
Settlement documentation

Detail of product offering including market share by product line
Inventory analysis including turnover, obsolescence and valuation policies
Backlog analysis by product line including analysis of seasonal issues
List of all major suppliers including dollar amount purchased per year

List of competitors and detail of market share
List of major clients
Analysis of pricing strategy
Current brochures and marketing materials
Sales commission structure
Sales projections by product line
Any pertinent marketing studies conducted by outside parties

Management organizational chart and bios of

senior personnel

Detail of any labor disputes

Employee compensation plans including pension, options, profit sharing, deferred compensation and retirement

Management incentive plans including pension, option, profit sharing, deferred compensation, retirement and any non-cash compensation

Employee confidentiality Agreements

Listing of any consulting Agreements

Number of employees, turnover, absentee problems and hiring projections

Employee HR, benefits, and insurance manuals

List of Company's Directors

Investigation report on all principals, managers, and directors

Credit history report on all principals, managers, and directors

Resume verification on all principals, managers, and directors

An appraisal of all equipment and fixed assets

List of all real property owned by the company

Copies of titles, mortgages, and deeds of trust

Detail of any easements or other encumbrances

Leases and sub-leases

Company space expansion plans

Patents, trademarks and other intangible assets

Detail all research and development in progress

Commercial analysis of R&D efforts

Documentation policies including examples

Copies of all past and planned company press

releases

Existing articles relating to the company and its industry

Company newsletters and any investor relations material

Any other information that might be pertinent to full disclosure of all company issues.

SAMPLE QUESTIONS FOR POTENTIAL INVESTMENT GROUPS

If are considering putting a putting together an investment group there are a few key questions that you should ask all potential investment group members.

1. Why are we investing?

2. How much do we want to invest?

3. How much should each group member contribute?

    a. How often?

4. How long do we want to invest?

5. Are we a closed group or are we open to all?

    a. When can new members join?

6. How do members exit the group?

7. What type of businesses do we want to support? (Be specific)

8. How do we make decisions? Unanimously? By majority? By executive committee?

9. What are our roles? Are we all equal? Are we electing representatives?

10. Do we want to work with advisors?

11. How often do we meet?

12. Where do we want to operate?

13. How do we pay out? Monthly? Quarterly? Annually?

There are lots of questions that will come from moving through these basic questions. Give yourselves time to thoughtfully consider and move through the questions.

BIBLIOGRAPHY

Works Cited

Bureau, U. C. (2019, Febrary 21). 1947, and 1952 to 2002 March Current Population Survey, 2003 to 2018 Annual Social and Economic Supplement to the Current Population Survey. Washington DC.

Hudson, M. (2017, December 1). Retrieved from Forbes: https://www.forbes.com/sites/mariannehudson/2017/12/01/in-depth-angel-investor-survey-sheds-light-on-angel-success/#3c6c480f7d35

Reuters. (2013, March 28). Retrieved from https://www.reuters.com/article/us-usa-stocks-sp-timeline/timeline-key-dates-and-milestones-in-the-sp-500s-history-idUS-BRE92R11Z20130328

Trends, S. B. (n.d.). Retrieved from https://www.embroker.com/blog/startup-statistics

Walker, J. E. (2009). *The history of black business in America: Capitalism, race, entrepreneurship.* UNC Press Books.

ACKNOWLEDGEMENT

Thank You to Greg Jackson for supporting my efforts, I love you. My business partners Dr. Carl Smart and Marlon Joris for trusting me to lead. To all the businessowners and entrepreneurs that have inspired me. Your work in the community is seen. Continue to be the Angels that make a difference for us all!

ABOUT THE AUTHOR

Dr. Shante Williams

About the Author DR. SHANTE P. WILLIAMS, MBA Dr. Shante Williams is currently the CEO of Black Pearl Global Investments, a $25M venture capital fund. She is a distinguished Venture Capitalist, business owner, Inventor, Intellectual Property Strategist, and Private Investor. In her career years, she has used her wealth of scientific knowledge as well as her passion for innovation to solve multiple complex problems across the industries of health, finance, and real estate. Best known for her creative problem-solving approach, Dr. Williams' impressive professional qualities and ethics make it easy for her to transition into various career paths seamlessly. Her proven track record of excellence and leadership has been an integral part of growth for many individuals and businesses. Before her current position, she worked fully in the medical field and is widely recognized for her stellar discovery of innovative chemotherapy treatments for high-grade invasive brain tumors. As soon as she discovers how to apply her innovative prowess to other facets of her industry, she earned numerous leadership positions. Shante was formerly the Vice President of Technology Acquisition in the Healthcare sector, the Director of Mergers and Acquisitions in the Consumer Healthcare Industry, even the Director of Intellectual Property in the Electric Drive Vehicle Industry. Having enjoyed remarkable years of accomplishment in Corporate America, she founded her first company, RW Capital Partners, which became an industry-leading firm specializing in Real Estate, Technology Development, Start-up/Stand-up, and Business Disputes Resolution. Her knowledge remains pivotal to helping entrepreneurs evolve and become more informed. She is a proud graduate of Winston-Salem State University (BS, Chemistry), The Ohio State University (PhD, in Integrated Biomedical Science specializing in Neuro-Oncology and Pharmacology), Queen's University of Charlotte (MBA). Dr. Williams has received numerous awards for her business and entrepreneurship efforts including 2020 Charlotte Inno Opportunity Champion award, 2019 Charlotte 50 Most Influential Women recognition, 2018 Athena International Young Professional Award, 2017 Alumni Achiever Award- Winston Salem State University,

2017 Charlotte Chamber Young Professional Entrepreneur Award Winner, 2017 Charlotte Business Journal 40 under 40 Award. In the venture capital sector, Dr. Williams continues to break barriers with Black Pearl's fund focused on reducing health disparities across the globe. Black Pearl is an advocate for those that continue to experience inferior outcomes and reduced access. Black Pearl's tag line "Be Well. Do Well." captures the firm's mission to invest in transformative companies around the world. Dr. Williams and her partners are seeking to change healthcare worldwide. Dr. Williams also serves the community as Chairman of the Board of Directors for the Charlotte Mecklenburg Black Chamber of Commerce and Heal Charlotte, a non-profit dedicated to holistic community change. Also, she is a Community Advisory Board Member for the local NPR affiliate WFAE 90.7, and a Community advisor for Shelter to Shutters a non-profit that deploys marketplace solutions to solve homelessness.

Made in the USA
Middletown, DE
11 March 2022